A man comes across an ancient enemy, beaten and left for dead. He lifts the wounded man onto the back of a donkey and takes him to an inn to tend to the man's recovery. Jesus tells this story and instructs those who are listening to "go and do likewise."

Likewise books explore a compassionate, active faith lived out in real time. When we're skeptical about the status quo, Likewise books challenge us to create culture responsibly. When we're confused about who we are and what we're supposed to be doing, Likewise books help us listen for God's voice. When we're discouraged by the troubled world we've inherited, Likewise books encourage us to hold onto hope.

In this life we will face challenges that demand our response. Likewise books face those challenges with us so we can act on faith.

LIKEWISE.   *Go and do.*

BLESSED ARE THE UNCOOL
Living Authentically in a World of Show

Paul Grant

IVP Books

An imprint of InterVarsity Press
Downers Grove, Illinois

InterVarsity Press
P.O. Box 1400, Downers Grove, IL 60515-1426
World Wide Web: www.ivpress.com
E-mail: email@ivpress.com

InterVarsity Press® is the book-publishing division of InterVarsity Christian Fellowship/USA®, a student movement active on campus at hundreds of universities, colleges and schools of nursing in the United States of America, and a member movement of the International Fellowship of Evangelical Students. For information about local and regional activities, write Public Relations Dept., InterVarsity Christian Fellowship/USA, 6400 Schroeder Rd., P.O. Box 7895, Madison, WI 53707-7895, or visit the IVCF website at <www.intervarsity.org>.

All Scripture quotations, unless otherwise indicated, are taken from Holy Bible, Today's New International Version™. Copyright ©2001 by International Bible Society. All rights reserved.

Design: cover: Matt Smith
       interior: Cindy Kiple
Images: Brent Larson/Fstop

ISBN-10: 0-8308-3603-9
ISBN-13: 978-0-8308-3603-1

Printed in the United States of America ∞

Library of Congress Cataloging-in-Publication Data

Grant, Paul, 1975 Sept. 9-
  Blessed are the uncool: living authentically in a world of show/
  Paul Grant.
      p. cm.—(A likewise book)
  Includes bibliographical references (p.   ).
  ISBN-13: 978-0-8308-3603-1 (pbk. alk. paper)
  ISBN-10: 0-8308-3603-9 (pbk. alk. paper)
  1. Self-perception—Religious aspects—Christianity. 2.
  Self-esteem—Religious aspects—Christianity. 3. Christianity and
  culture. I. Title.

  BV4598.25.G74 2006
  248.4—dc22

                                                                    2006030473

P	18	17	16	15	14	13	12	11	10	9	8	7	6	5	4	3	2
Y	20	19	18	17	16	15	14	13	12	11	10	09	08	07				

For Dad, who taught me faith
For Mom, who taught me hope
For Becca, who taught me love

CONTENTS

PART ONE

The Trouble with Cool

1

YOU GOT TO WEAR YOUR SUNGLASSES

Our Obsession, Others' Profit

NOT COOL

Admit it: you want to be cool.

On your way home from work, canned ghetto-rage from a neighboring car pounds syncopated coolness through your windshield. Suddenly you feel uncool and you hate the feeling. So you lean back in your seat and put a meaner look on your face, in case the car-stereo guy glances over and sees you.

You go to a party, and you're greeted with songs that reduce you to a piece of meat. But nobody else seems to mind, so you don't leave, even when they start showing pornography on the big screen. After all, you don't want to look like you don't get it.

Maybe you buy magazines and listen to music you don't even like because you're afraid of being out of the loop. Maybe you ingratiate yourself to rude jerks because you want them to think you're cool. Maybe as a teenager you starved yourself skinny because it was the thing to do; and now as an adult it's no longer cool to hurt yourself, but you can't stop.

You know better than this; with your head you understand that this insecurity has no basis in reality. But your gut is way ahead of your mind on this one, driven by deeply rooted ghosts of shame, fear and loneliness.

This book is about those ghosts. It's about *cool*.

Cool is all around us, saturating our culture. We can't escape it. Cool informs both our mundane activities and our significant decisions. It is an attitude, a habit, a worldview, a feeling. Sometimes we control cool, but sometimes it controls us. And sometimes, cool reduces us to extras in somebody else's fantasy—passers-by to whom he or she can feel superior.

Cool appears in myriad and contradictory forms.

- Teenage rebellion provokes the adult world's fears of irrelevance.
- The for-profit advertising world sells images of cool to exploit our insecurities.
- The jaded, cynical response to advertising, an anti-cool, ultimately is the same animal in a different hide.
- There's even cool Christianity: a resolute disassociation from embarrassing churches or older Christians.

I've been around cool my whole life, like just about everyone else in today's world, sometimes observing cool from a distance, and sometimes, in spite of myself, trying wholeheartedly to be cool. I was born in the western United States into a healthy family. Cool was not a value in my home, but authentic and courageous action most certainly was. My parents were young enough that by the time I wanted to be cool, they could remember cool's appeal and were able to uncover cool delusions for me.

When I was nine, my family left the United States for a seven-year missionary stint in Switzerland. There I lived an exciting urban life in a profoundly multiethnic world. We lived in the metropolis of Zurich during my adolescent years, before returning to the States in the early 1990s.

My relationship with cool was fairly standard through my early grades in school, which is to say I lived in it, near it and aware of it. Everything changed for me in an instant, however, midway through a chewing-out at the hands of my high school Latin teacher.

Nothing says "establishment" quite like Latin class, and at my school eight semesters were required. My friends and I were typical teenagers to Herr Roth, antagonizing him at every opportunity. One day I pushed him over the edge. When class was dismissed, he pulled me into the hallway. I was terrified, but with all the other kids walking by, I needed to compose myself quickly. The man yelled at me for twenty minutes straight. I can only guess what he was saying—probably things like "You're wasting your life"—because I wasn't really listening. I was too busy demonstrating, via body language, that I didn't care how angry he was.

Then it happened. Suddenly I realized, *I'm trying to be cool.*

At that moment, I understood that cool doesn't reside in objects or people; it is a tool that can be wielded. Furthermore, I understood that this was an incredible and possibly dangerous secret to power and influence. More thought was needed, so I wiped the smirk off my face and let Herr Roth finish. It worked. He calmed down within seconds of feeling that he was being listened to.

It was as if scales had fallen out of my eyes. The entire world (which is to say, the entire high school scene) felt different. I could manipulate people with something as simple as body language—and I could just as easily be manipulated. On that day, cool became a subject of my curiosity.

Cool is a tool that can be wielded.

I've had my eyes wide open since that moment with Herr Roth. I have learned that cool is far more powerful than we realize, and that like the ring of power in J. R. R. Tolkien's *Lord of the Rings,* most of us don't have the mental strength to wield it. More often, cool wields us.

Cool is not innocent. Cool is the sunglasses we wear so people don't see that we're lonely, frightened or ashamed. It can alienate us from community, family and God. We're so attuned to cool that we can hardly imagine life without it.

This book is an attempt to imagine such a life: it is a search for a better way, an *uncool* we can live with; an *uncool* that will free us up to live healthy, authentic lives.

TO DEFINE IS TO LIMIT

But *what is* cool anyway? For a passion so prominent in our hearts, we barely notice it, or think about it. We watch our tempers, we control our appetites, and we surrender our jealousies to God, but cool flies below our radar. Where did it come from? How does it affect our community? What does cool want? Is it merely a hangover from adolescence? Or is it something bigger?

One of the difficulties in defining cool is the word's near omnipresence in contemporary American English. We say "cool" as a generic term of approval. It can mean spontaneous, clever, slick, fashionable, high-tech, successful or original. Cool is a compliment; "That's cool," in fact, was the most common response people had when I told them I was writing this book.

Cool is

the private

performance of

rebellion for

rebellion's sake.

In their book *Cool Rules: Anatomy of an Attitude,* Dick Pountain and David Robins supply a definition for cool: *an attitude of permanent, private rebellion*. I think this needs to be taken further. In this book I am defining cool as *the private performance of rebellion for rebellion's sake.*

First of all, cool is *private*. It is individualistic from beginning to end, even when small groups of in-the-know insiders are involved: even in tight-knit cliques, membership is less about faithful friendship and looking out for each other, and more about excluding outsiders.

Second, cool is a *performance*. Cool exists to show off to an uncool audience. And since performance is always immediate, cool does not care about yesterday or tomorrow, only about right now.

Third, cool is about *rebellion*. Cool communicates categorical disrespect for authority. Cool accepts no limits on behavior and no limits on identity, insisting instead on an individual authority to define one-self, and to know others without being known. That's why sunglasses are cool. They allow the wearers to look at the world without reveal-ing who they are.

Finally, cool's rebellion is *for its own sake*. There are many reasons that people rebel, from injustice to petty disagreements, but normal rebellion ends when the conflict is resolved. Not so with cool: cool shows universal contempt for authority, extending across all space and time: Cool is never done being cool. Since this contempt for au-thority applies to tradition and current affairs alike, we can say that cool exists outside of time.

In the long run—the view from eternity—living only for the mo-ment is less than shallow: it's inhuman. We are created for commu-nity, for family, for spiritual life, all of which relate to the past and the future. Real relationships extend backward in time (our memories) and forward into the future (our hopes and fears). Living for the mo-ment is an obstacle to spiritual and social health. Basically, whether pursued individually or collectively, cool is antisocial.

African American teenagers, white frat boys, gospel singers, ath-letes and French rioters can all embody mutually exclusive strains of cool but have a story in com-mon: *the private performance of rebellion for rebel-lion's sake*. This story is important if we are to un-derstand cool, since a person or group determined to be cool will shrug off attempts to understand them. In *A Portrait of Dorian Gray*, Oscar Wilde's Henry Wotton responds to a simple question—"What are you?"—in a decidedly twenty-first century way: "To define is to limit." In other words, if you find out who I am, you might be able to call my bluff. The self-assured hipster may be re-vealed as a scared and lonely kid. The rebel without a cause may be exposed as a senseless car crash waiting to happen.

Cool is never done being cool.

If we are going to live whole, healthy lives, we're going to have to step away from the shame and fear we hide behind cool. Authentic faith is uncool in the sense that it is unashamed. Christians are far richer than the empty bravado behind cool because our story is a great story: a God dies to give us life in abundance. And once we've begun to live uncool, our story will get ever sweeter.

THE STORY OF COOL

The story of cool is, to a significant extent, the story of race in America. From the slave economy and the industrial revolution, to the Civil Rights movement and the cultural revolutions of the sixties, to twenty-first century pop culture, American cool and American racism were born together and have grown up together. Cool as we know it was born at the shadowy intersection of black and white America, as African slaves (and later, African Americans) asserted their humanity against vehement white assertions to the contrary: *"The circumstances we find ourselves in are absurd."* One slave spiritual asserted humanity and God's justice at once, in a manner that could not have been un-threatening to slaveholders:

> Didn't my Lord deliver Daniel,
> And why not every man?

In the twentieth century, as racism emerged as slavery's successor, W. E. B. Du Bois would write:

> It is a particular sensation, this double-consciousness, this sense of always looking at oneself through the eyes of others. . . . One ever feels his two-ness,—an American, a Negro, two thoughts, two unreconciled strivings; two warring ideals in one dark body, whose dogged strength alone keeps it from being torn asunder. The history of the American Negro is the history of this strife—this longing . . . to merge his double self into a better and truer self.

In some cases African Americans flipped this courageous resistance against exclusion into an inverted exclusion: *"You whites may think you're in control, but I see a bigger picture, and thus I am more in control than you are."* Several splinter groups of the Nation of Islam, for instance, have held that black people are gods and whites are devils.

Poor whites, themselves outsiders in the predominant society and often barely removed from peasantry and slavery themselves, recognized the language of supremacy being communicated by blacks and responded in kind, offering their own version of exclusionary assertion. Kathleen Neal Cleaver explains from the example of Irish immigrants:

> Early in the nineteenth century, it was an open question among the native born white Protestants whether these Celtic immigrants belonged to the white race. . . . The imperative driving Irish workers to define themselves as whites, despite their hatred of the British and distaste for their American descendants, was that "public and psychological wage" that whiteness promised to desperate immigrants in an industrializing society that held them in contempt.

The poorest of the whites were the ones with the most day-to-day contact with blacks. White fear of interracial marriage, among other factors, caused racial tension to intensify in the early twentieth century.

In such an environment jazz emerged. Secular, sexual and drawing a large white audience, it is no surprise jazz was divisive—the object of parental terror and youthful rebellion. Cool came into its own in the Jazz Age between the first and second World Wars; after rock and roll gave whites a cool music that sounded much more familiar to their ears, things really got going.

By the early 1960s, American youth were sold on cool, and advertisers began to sell it to them. Thomas Frank notes, in *The Conquest of*

Cool: "The ads . . . had an uncanny ability to cut through the over-blown advertising rhetoric of the 1950s . . . to appeal directly to the powerful but unmentionable public fears of conformity, of manipulation, of fraud, and of powerlessness, and to sell products by so doing."

Advertising nurtured a new—and particularly potent—permutation of cool: radical individualism. Frank continues, "The basic task . . . [is] not to encourage conformity but a never-ending rebellion against whatever it is that everyone else is doing, a forced and exaggerated individualism." A better descriptor of cool would be hard to find, yet Frank is talking about corporate capitalism.

ADVERTISING AND ISOLATION

Today most people's contact with cool comes through mass media and consumer society. But such contact is fleeting; cool's power lies in part in its inscrutability—it's gone the second you reach it. Cultural observers say that we live in a day and age in which our very identities are only surfaces. And when we live superficially—when we live only in the moment, when we are what we consume—we put ourselves at the disposal of whoever has the courage to wield the past and the ambition to shape the future. Advertisers convince us of our ignorance so that they can add mystery to their products.

Cool's power lies in part in its inscrutability. Cool is the most powerful spiritual environment possible for advertisers. Not even the cradle or the marriage bed are off-limits to marketing campaigns. All relations—save those involving brand-loyalty—are subjected to the coolness of rebellion. We are communal creatures, but advertisers target *individuals,* because individuals—all alone in the world, or at least the store—are more susceptible to messages of being incomplete without the consumer product in question. It is by dividing communities into collections of individuals that advertisers conquer consumer resistance.

Communities *identify* via their clothes; consumers *individuate* via clothes. Communities make their own music; individual consumers buy it. Communities don't require half the commodities needed by collections of individuals. Cool marketing thus sells the image of belonging to, and inclusion in, the product being sold, rather than a real community. For example, whereas the standards for beauty are rooted in memory and thus community, fashion offers an individualized consumer product (such as an item of clothing) that brands its wearers with supposed status and wealth.

Similarly, cool sexuality prefers pornography to love. Pamela Paul writes, "Many women today, particularly college students, consider the production and consumption of pornography a form of sex-positive activism." Cool sexuality is a bizarre combination of control and libertarianism. Real love is about more than one person and more than one moment, whereas porn is all about control. I can turn on the computer and turn it off whenever I want; I can control the relationship on my own terms.

Real love is about other people, and therefore by definition not about control. As the Song of Songs says, "Love is as strong as death, its jealousy unyielding as the grave. It burns like blazing fire, like a mighty fire" (Song of Songs 8:6). Love—real love—is in a whole other league than cool. Cool cares less about love and more about freedom. The fact that societies establish sexual boundaries to protect men, women and children doesn't bother cool. Cool rebels against all boundaries— even the ultimate boundary of death.

Cool rebels against all boundaries— even the ultimate boundary of death.

Ever since the Garden of Eden, death has been a primary human preoccupation. The greatest story ever told is that Jesus' sacrifice on the cross gives us the power to transcend death. But thinking about the cross also connects us with Jesus' defeat and humiliation. Can anyone seriously remain cool while meditating on a grisly crucifixion? Gangster fantasies like rapper 50 Cent's project coolness by offering more fashionable, sexier myths of overcoming death. In "Many Men (Wish Death)," from the album *Get Rich or Die Tryin'*, 50 Cent writes:

> Many men wish death upon me . . .
> Better watch how you talk, when you talk about me
> 'Cause I'll come and take your life away.

He makes the point more bluntly in the song "50 Bars": "When I'm dead and gone, n—— gonna remember my name 50." In other words, death can't stop me.

Some pronounced the end of cool cynicism in the aftermath of the terrorist attacks on America on September 11, 2001. Cynicism is a luxury for peacetime, the reasoning went. Even the satirical weekly *The Onion* dropped publication for a week.

But cool cynicism is harder to hijack than a mere airplane. Cool cynicism is a cult of insider knowledge. In a world where everything is for sale, cool cynicism protects itself by refusing to belong to anyone or anything. In 2006 Wal-Mart announced it would begin selling organically grown produce. The hostile response from people who would otherwise celebrate such a giant step for the environmental movement demonstrates two things: first, it's easier to be against something than for its alternative; second and more important, something cool—say, eating organic food—becomes less cool when it's embraced by something uncool—say, Wal-Mart.

Cynicism culminates in contempt for just about everything relationally good. Anticapitalist Kalle Lasn calls it "the dark side of cool":

> It's part of the reason we watch too much TV and don't bother to vote. It's why we get stuck year after year in tedious, meaningless jobs. It's why we're bored so much of the time and be-

come compulsive shoppers. To find a way out of cynicism is to find a way out of the postmodern malaise. On the far side of cynicism lies freedom.

Ultimately, Lasn says, "Cool is the opiate of our time, and . . . we have grown dependent on it to maintain our identities." Real people are never cool; only their projected identities are. Smooth guys far too often have child support to pay. Fine dressers are often broke, party animals look a whole lot better at midnight than at four, and a lot of world-traveling backpackers are really just hiding from their parents.

> **Real people are never cool; only their projected identities are.**

Cool interferes with relationships and communities. Cool is "powerlessness, disconnection and shame." The key word here is *shame*. Cool is about performance: if you act uncool in public, the trendiest clothes won't help you. Peer pressure is a social device for enforcing conformity; the cool kids at a high school are not necessarily the rebels. They may well be the rich kids, the athletes or exclusive cliques such as the "Plastics" in the film *Mean Girls*.

In the film, Lindsey Lohan's character is dropped into the teenage jungle of bourgeois Evanston, Illinois, after having spent most of her life in the tropical jungles of "Africa," a faraway place never fully defined. Lohan's parents are white scientists; her mother has taken a tenure-track job at Northwestern University.

Lohan initially observes her high school's cliques with an outsider's eye. As the only character capable of moving between groups, she is the only truly "cool" character in the film. She quickly throws her whole self into a decidedly insider project: dethroning the Plastics. Along the way she "loses her cool"—she begins to wear the Plastics' persona, and the persona begins to wear her.

Peer pressure demands that everyone be the same. The implicit threat in peer pressure is humiliation: if you don't dress like us or behave like us, we will shame you. But cool is more exclusive; being cool is less about conformity to the fashions of the day than about being the only one or ones in the know.

Cool starts off in rebellion but ends up in a mess. Lasn likens it to an addictive drug:

> Cool is indispensable—and readily, endlessly dispersed. You can get it on every corner (for the right price), though it's highly addictive and its effects are short-lived. If you're here for cool today, you'll almost certainly be back for more tomorrow.

Meanwhile, others are laughing their way to the bank. Take a look at TV, for instance. Big businesses don't do anything if there's no profit to be made. Yet televised entertainment still comes to your home for free. Where is the money?

The viewing public is not the industry's primary customers. Loyal viewers, as measured by Nielsen ratings, are a commodity networks sell to advertising corporations. The more viewers the network can promise, and the more demographic information the network knows about those viewers, the higher the advertising rates the network can command.

The trouble is that after a while, the viewing public develops immunity to ads. We no longer believe the message that we need the advertised product. This consumer resistance forces advertisers to come up with new strategies for disorienting consumers' psychological defenses. For years, for instance, business philosophers have advocated product "branding" as a way of bypassing critical consumer thought. But branding gradually loses its juice—consumers reclaim their critical faculties. So business thinkers such as Kevin Roberts suggest getting consumers to fall in love with the products being sold.

And on it goes. When the mind is no longer a strategic battleground for the consumer's pocketbook, go for the gut. When the gut doesn't work, go for the heart. In a marketplace such as this, with fragmented consumers, permanent rebellion becomes a reasonable response. Cool can feel like a safe harbor. That's exactly why cool is the advertising El Dorado. Whoever owns cool owns the others. As long as advertisers can convince consumers that certain consumer products contain a coolness that eludes them, advertisers have the upper hand. Cool binds us to the products we buy, all the while preventing us from developing fully human relationships.

THE POWER OF LOVE

Cool contains enough contradictions and illusions to make one's head spin. But those afterparty moments of honesty, when we know—*really know*—that we're lost and going nowhere, are moments of opportunity. Weakness, not success, is our way out. When we feel lonely and vulnerable—when we feel uncool—God is inviting us to a whole life. When we look around and ask, "What am I doing with my life?" we can begin to live real lives.

> When we feel lonely and vulnerable— when we feel uncool—God is inviting us to a whole life.

We moved to Wisconsin while I was still in high school, and though I initially resisted—Wisconsin is far less cool than Zurich—I grew to enjoy the place, to the point where I am still here fourteen years later, while the rest of my family has returned to our homeland in the intermountain American west.

I went to college in Madison, at the University of Wisconsin. This large Big Ten school is one of the country's most politically active, and is also one of the country's most debauched party schools. Study hard, party hard, the campus culture says. The UW is thus an easy place to figure yourself out, if you don't smoke your brains out first. I believe I chose the former.

In an environment dedicated to "ever encourag[ing] that fearless sifting and winnowing by which alone the truth can be found"—that's the motto of the UW—I discovered that Jesus' offer of "life to the full"

(John 10:10) and Paul's message that it was "for freedom that Christ has set us free" (Galatians 5:1) were far more compelling and life-giving than the cool culture around me. I found the beloved community of the church.

Here then is the crossroads we face: a cool moment, or a freeing, healthy life in Christ. We can't have both. The church's greatest power lies in its being the "beloved community"—the supernatural community created by none other than God himself through his Spirit. God's love is the most deep-feeling, creative force in the universe, and the incredible truth is that this love lives in the church. In its sharing of Christ's suffering, and in its practice of inclusive hospitality, the beloved community displays cool's fundamental phoniness to the world. Cool in one corner, and the love God gives his followers in the other? It's not even a fair fight. The beloved community shatters cool's rebellion.

As God's people living out the full life Jesus promised, the freedom Paul claimed for us, the beloved community must escape the cult of cool. We're so used to pursuing cool that being uncool is scary. But what other honest option do we have? We have been given Jesus' words of life, and stewarding those words in a world suffering the effects of cool is a serious matter. Jesus proved his kingship by dying as a contemptible criminal. Following his example, we can and must die to ourselves. We must die to cool. But when we open our hearts for Christ's sake, we will live authentically: at the level of human suffering, as theologian Ray Aldred has said, because that is where God's power is greatest. The sooner we understand the impossibility of the church's being simultaneously cool and authentic, the better.

When we open our hearts for Christ's sake, we will gain authenticity. God calls us sons and daughters. He can protect us and make us whole. He can make us into a family. Christian love is vulnerability before God, which for all its uncoolness is the very substance of abundant life, love and worship.

Love, not cool, is a life worth living.

2

REBELLION ON STAGE

Definitions and Contradictions

I was walking back to school after lunch. A mixed company of teenagers sat on a stoop a few yards ahead to my left. I was powerfully conscious of the gendered atmospheric tension, as these beautiful, cool and mature people (none older than sixteen) engaged each other in flirtatious bravado. They were smoking cigarettes.

Anonymity was my best friend. I could have walked by unnoticed, but I really wanted to be noticed, especially by the girls. I slid one arm out from my backpack's shoulder straps, to hang the bag like the big kids did. I unzipped my jacket, and tried to strike a cool pose.

What end result was I looking for? Did I want to be called out by the teenagers to come join them? Did I want a girlfriend? Or a smoke? None of the above, probably. I was a few years away from any interest in girls, beyond the theoretical; as for smoking I was convinced, courtesy of a *Boy's Life* article on drugs, that a single cigarette would give me lung cancer. I had already tremblingly said no to a classmate's first offer of a puff.

God only knows what outcome I wanted, but at least a dozen people saw the outcome I got: a street sign in my face. Not once, but twice.

Right in front of the stoop, I walked into a pole. Although my nose was pointed straight ahead, my eyes, ears and mind were on that stoop, checking to see if I was being watched. Suddenly I existed for the teenagers—but only as an object of uproar. They exploded with laughter, high fives and lots of words in some foreign language. In every conceivable way, I was out, and they were in.

In a last-ditch effort to preserve my dignity, I shrugged off the incident, ignored my smarting nose, and continued down the street—with an eagle eye to the left, observing their jeers. I paid close enough attention that—unbelievably—I walked into the next sign, scarcely twelve feet on. I didn't wait for the teenagers' reaction: I fled the scene as fast as I could run. I had to run before I started to cry. Perhaps I could run fast enough to catch that ever-elusive cool.

THE WORLD IS A STAGE

Philosophers might at least half-seriously debate whether a tree falling in the forest makes a noise if no one is there to hear it. But not so with cool. Without an audience, there simply is no cool.

But an audience alone can't guarantee cool. It can't be banked. If you were cool yesterday, that means nothing today. Cool is a fair-weather friend: when trouble comes, cool takes off without a second's thought, and you're left high and dry.

Without an audience, there simply is no cool. For generations now, police, parents and high school principals have tried to suppress cool without much success. But if you take away its audience, cool disappears into thin air, because cool is a both a mood and an attitude—though in a slightly different sense from everyday language.

Mood. Philosopher Lars Svendsen describes *mood* as the social environment in which perception, emotions and thoughts may occur: "It is basically via a mood that we relate to our surroundings."

An army recruit at boot camp can't be cool because the mood is not right. Drill sergeants are not remotely inclined to tolerate a recruit's individualized performance (unless it's a performance in personal humiliation); likewise, fellow recruits have learned not to provoke the drill sergeant and consequently are too terrified to provide an audience. The recruit's world is under the drill sergeant's domain. At home, in contrast, the authorities—high school, police and parents—exert a limited power; where an audience could possibly materialize, a cool performer dare not drop his pose.

Attitude. If cool requires a receptive audience, the main piece of the performance is *attitude*—a projection of mastery over the entire environment. Cool glories in the spotlight, saying "I am better than you. I am an individual; you are a clone. I know what's really going on here; you don't. I can get out of here; you can't."

Cool is more about performance than measurable accomplishment. This is why the pantheon of cool is so disproportionately populated with artists. Miles Davis, Madonna, Tupac Shakur, Dennis Rodman, Marilyn Monroe, O. J. Simpson, James Dean and even Ché Guevara were all in the first instance *performers*. Their actual skills on stage or in the arena mattered less than the way they worked the crowd and got under the skin of their opponents.

There are two distinct Ché Guevaras: the real Latin American revolutionary and the North American poster boy, with ruggedly dashing looks, a militant beret and gentle but determined eyes. Generations of Latin Americans have held Ché up as an angel come to earth to free the masses; meanwhile, generations of North American college students have held him up as an icon, giving the middle finger to *the man*.

Dennis Rodman was often surrounded by multiple superior players on the basketball court, including the game's all-time greatest, Michael Jordan. Yet Rodman managed to draw all eyes to himself. Cool can't be proven a *loser*, even when cool *loses* in real terms.

Celebrities are not inherently cool. But since our culture values performance above goodness or wisdom, we disproportionately *celebrate* performers. And since cool dominates our culture, *cool performers* are the most celebrated.

REBELLION AND PROPHECY

One of the primary vehicles of cool performance is rebellion—albeit a particular (and relatively toothless) breed of rebellion. Ché (the poster boy version) stands eternally in rebellion. He doesn't actually get down to the business of building a new society, or administering sustainable justice. (Perhaps that's why Ché, gunned down in his youth, remains far more popular than his buddy Fidel Castro.) Cool rebels can't build a new world because their commitment to the cause is surpassed by their commitment to rebellion. The "revolution" of cool rebellion is an individual affair, requiring no selfless sacrifice.

Not all rebellion is wrong, of course, and not all individual rebellion is about being cool. In contrast to the street peformance of cool, which has no higher goal than looking good in the moment, there is a kind of rebellion practiced by the prophets.

Prophets are messengers from God, messengers against wrongdoing in a government or a society. Prophets are almost universally rejected or worse. The most famous biblical example of a prophet's loneliness is Elijah's complaint to God in 1 Kings 19. Elijah had just achieved the greatest victory of his career. He had challenged 450 Baal prophets to a fiery demonstration of God's power. He had spoken to a humiliated king, and he had witnessed rain return to the countryside after a lengthy drought. Never had more people listened to his message. But what did it get him? He had to run for his life; they were coming to get him. Now a refugee in his own country, he began to beg God to let him die. God hears him out.

> I have been very zealous for the LORD God Almighty. The Israelites have rejected your covenant, torn down your altars, and put the prophets to death with the sword. I am the only one left, and now they are trying to kill me. (1 Kings 19:10)

Elijah is voicing three complaints at once: that his efforts have nothing to show for themselves; that he is alone; and that he is in danger for his life.

The Israelites had rejected the covenant. This was not a new problem; it was what had led Elijah into his role in the first place. God doesn't answer this complaint. He doesn't answer the third complaint, either. People were out to kill Elijah, but God offers no promise of security.

God does, however respond to Elijah's second complaint, "I am the only one." Throughout the Bible, we see that loneliness is a very serious matter for God. In Elijah's case, God does not promise life for him, but he does give him a friend. God tells Elijah to go to a certain place, where he will find his successor Elisha. God also informs Elijah of seven thousand people who remain faithful to God. In other words, God addresses Elijah's personal loneliness, and promises that his individual rebellion is not as individual as it seems.

Except in rare cases such as Elijah's, God expects us all to live in community. This is not because he wants to limit us. It is because human nature is communal. Human nature is communal because we are created in God's image, and God is love. Far more than individual experiences, vision quests and the like, spiritual reality finds its basis in community. Cool—or private—rebellion, when it gets down to it, is not merely lame and ultimately unbearable. It's also plain old boring.

Loneliness is a very serious matter for God.

Sometimes we have to act on our own, out of the conviction that history is on our side. But there is a world of difference between the lonely rebellion of a prophet, and the rebellion-for-rebellion's-sake of the hipster. Prophets don't want to be alone; their greatest desire is to work themselves out of a job. Prophets stand alone against evil, for instance, but hope that everyone else will quickly join them. Cool rebels, on the other hand, don't want to be joined by the world; that will just force them to find another means of standing apart.

Normal wars are fought with an end to war in mind. Not so with cool. Nothing is theoretically sufficient to persuade the hipster to lay down arms: not love, not God, not justice or injustice, artistic fulfillment or eternal peace can make the permanent rebel give up his striving against the world. For cool, rebellion itself is the cause. The only option, aside from giving up, is to continue forever.

Cool rebellion sets itself outside of history—rebellion with no beginning and no end. John Leland, whose *Hip: The History* is for the most part a hymnal to the praises of individualism, proudly announces

> the emancipation of the present tense, which now informs every new product or advertisement. . . . It undermines the authority of work, school, church and family, which all demand that we subordinate the present to the future.

But all time is not relative: there is a real story behind cool. Cool may have forgotten where it came from; cool may pretend to have no daddy. But it can't hide from the truth forever.

THE AFRICAN ORIGINS OF AMERICAN COOL

For most of its American career, cool has been associated with rebellion of one sort or another. That doesn't tell us much, because the whole of American history is almost a sequence of continuous rebellion. In his marvelous book *This Rebellious House*, Steven Keillor suggests that defiance of authority is the essential theme of American history: "paradoxically . . . the Christianity carried by Europeans to the New World was divinely revealed truth, yet those who carried it were in serious rebellion against it." Cool has always been the shadow figure in American church history, suggesting itself as a proud alternative to bending the knee before God or earthly powers.

Pountain and Robins contend that "modern Cool may represent the survival and adaptation of such attitudes as transported to

America and Europe by the slave trade." Art historian Robert Farris Thompson traces cool's origins to the belly of a slave ship: "Cool
or *itetu* contained meanings of conciliation and gentleness of character, the ability to defuse fights and disputes, of generosity and
grace." *Itetu* is a concept from the Yoruba language of West Africa,
conveying strength and performance under pressure. It's a positive
and communal value. If you whip out a meal for your friends without making a big deal about it, that's *itetu*. If you can defuse a hostile
crowd, that's *itetu*.

Itetu enabled slaves to assert their humanity in inhuman circumstances. "Cool afforded [plantation slaves] a symbolic territory beyond the jurisdiction of their white owners." Cool was thus an assertion of superiority to slave masters' choreography of degradation.

Hip entered the American lexicon thanks to the Wolof (Senegal)
words *hepi* ("to see") or *hipi* ("to open one's eyes"). Leland explains:

> From the start . . . *hip* is a term of *enlightenment*. . . . The slaves
> also brought the Wolof *dega* ("to understand"), source of the
> colloquial *dig*. . . . Hip begins, then, as a subversive intelligence
> that outsiders developed under the eye of insiders. It was one of
> the tools Africans developed to negotiate an alien landscape.

Slave economies worked double-time to undermine slave community, and so what began as a skill for preserving the peace in a social
setting became a tool for preserving one's own internal peace. Many
highly educated Africans—royal attendants, astrologers, translators,
historians, accountants and even professors—ended their days at the
receiving end of a whip wielded by an English, Portuguese or American brute, who was himself often too stupid for a career in any field
but brutishness. Christian slaves learned to see their suffering in the
big picture of God's hand in history. God sent his Holy Spirit to slave
congregations, giving them spiritual fruit and spiritual power. As the
traditional spiritual song goes,

This joy that I have,
The world didn't give it to me,
The world didn't give it and the world can't take it away.

White observers misunderstood this joy amidst suffering as stupidity. But these songs contextualized the Christian hope of slaves into their African heritage and their present circumstances, and thus served as a foundation for what would become a distinctive American music form.

WHITE TRANSFORMATION OF COOL

Once it reached American shores, *hepi* could not remain an exclusively black performance. If Africans weren't cultural blank slates, neither were the Europeans they encountered in the new world. America's very soul was emerging in that crosscultural experience. In 1953, from a remote mountain village in Europe, where he was the first black person to ever set foot, James Baldwin wrote:

> The time has come to realize that the interracial drama acted out on the American continent has not only created a new black man, it has created a new white man, too. . . . One of the things that distinguishes Americans from other people is that no other people have been so deeply involved in the lives of black men, and visa-versa. . . . This world is white no longer, and it will never be white again.

In other words, white Americans are who they are because of their common history with black Americans. Even American church music, in genres from contemporary worship to rock-infused hymns, to gospel funk, is profoundly multiracial. Listen to pop radio or country or rock, or even any of several American classical compositions: call-and-response is there. Syncopation is there. Blues chords are there. And cool is there.

Whites also transformed cool, however, creating a genuinely new beast in the process. The prevailing worldview of the West is wrapped up in Enlightenment myths of progress and human goodness. Humans pronounced themselves the measure of all things, to the exclusion of divine revelation. We came to believe we could fix everything ourselves—including ourselves. The ills of society could be corrected by reforming or replacing systems—not monarchies but democracies, not popes but the priesthood of all believers, not mysticism but materialism, not a divine-human Christ but a historical Jesus. We are heirs of a multicentury-long project, begun in Europe, to create a society free from the authority of kings and priests—free even from the authority of God.

John Leland locates the first conscious white appropriation of African cool in the nineteenth century, when Walt Whitman, Herman Melville and Henry Thoreau began to ascribe to Euro-American individualism an almost mystical power. The "Lost Generation" of young whites in the 1920s listened to jazz and picked up black dances like the Charleston in a day when immigration was being aggressively curtailed and the social segregation of the races reached its high-water mark.

THE COLLAPSE OF COOL

Cool serves as a means of covering up the shame of our history and our fear for the future, but taken to its logical conclusion, cool's two possible ends are boredom or collapse. No one has better described cool's historical problem than Norman Mailer in his 1957 essay *The White Negro*.

> The Second World War presented a mirror to the human condition which blinded anyone who looked into it. . . . If society was so murderous, then who could ignore the most hideous questions about his own nature? . . . The only life-giving answer

is . . . to divorce oneself from society, to exist without roots . . .
[to exist] in that enormous present which is without past or future, memory or planned intention.

From the atrocities of World War II to today's genocides and human trafficking, cool sees nothing but pain behind and no reason for
hope ahead, and so cool lives in the here and now. But living for the
moment is death to aspiration, dreams, relationships and creativity.
As Lars Svendsen explains in *The Philosophy of Boredom*, cool quickly
gives way to boredom, a characteristic feature of the modern world
with roots that go back to the Greek concept *acedia*, one of the ancient
church's seven deadly sins:

> [Acedia] contains a rejection of—or rather detestation of—God
> and his creation. *Acedia* is the diametric opposite of the joy one
> ought to feel toward God and his works. . . . Such an approach
> is unsatisfactory because it overlooks the possibility that the
> outside world—rather than the person—is
> the problem, or disallows that the world
> plays any role at all. Boredom is not just a
> phenomenon that afflicts individuals; it is,
> to just as great an extent, a social and cul-
> tural phenomenon.

Cool sees nothing but pain behind and no reason for hope ahead.

Boredom is sometimes a mood in our hearts or
our communities or even our churches, but at its
core, boredom is the refusal to take delight in the world that God has
made.

GENERATION GAPS AND BELOVED COMMUNITY

Despite its intrinsic hopelessness and detachment from the world,
cool rebellion wraps itself around the faith of countless young Christians. They might claim righteous causes, but for many the underly-

ing motivation is that it feels good to rebel.

Really though, don't all youth rebel? Every generation struggles with its parents. A degree of painful separation, of youthful rebellion, is a basic aspect of development. But while parent-child conflict may be as old as the human race, cool has taken it to a whole new level. Cool can be a powerful but subterranean motivation, and a closer look at cool Christianity begins to turn up some decidedly unfortunate qualities, including shame, disunity and idolatry.

There's another way of doing life. The world God has created is deeply emotional. Throughout Scripture, we are rarely let in on God's line of reasoning, but we are always appraised of his emotional state. He expresses deep hurt in the face of disloyalty, comparing it to marital infidelity: "What can I do with you, Judah? Your love is like the morning mist, like the early dew that disappears" (Hosea 6:4). His response to injustice is not legalistically cool but emotionally hot: "Away with the noise of your songs! I will not listen to the music of your harps. But let justice roll on like a river, righteousness like a never-failing stream!" (Amos 5:23-24). Elsewhere he reveals himself as deeply grieving, compassionate, disappointed, joyful, hopeful, ecstatic, despairing and boiling angry. God is relational all the way down, and authentic emotions seem to be his primary interface with his people. God never poses or puts on. God loves—with the love of a mother for her children, the love of a lover for her beloved, or in Jesus' case, the love of a child for his Father.

God is relational all the way down.

Christianity is a radically relational and historical faith. Cool lives in the here and now, but the beloved community finds its sense of belonging in shared memory and tradition. It is focused on a moment in space and time, the moment of *Immanuel,* God-with-us. Theologian Mark Medley has observed that the Lord's Supper subvert[s] false identities marketed to us . . . by giving us a new identity as members of God's very body. . . . When we open our hands to God in Christ in order to receive the gift of grain and fruit, as well as the gift of our true identity, we must also open our hands to others. Otherwise, we do violence to the very life-giving mystery at the heart of the church's life.

We cannot live as Christians without each other. Because of the model we have of Jesus' sacrifice on the cross, we can take courage as we take a hard look at cool. We can survive the loss of our cool because our faith is rooted in the compassion of the God who is *Immanuel,* God-with-us. The beloved community empowers us to feel feelings, where once we could only feel cool. The loneliness of cool rebellion is met by the church in the gift of reconciliation.

3

THE CAUCASIAN STORMS HARLEM

Culture and Community

In the fall of 2005, Hurricane Katrina blew into New Orleans. Katrina was big—the biggest American natural disaster in living memory—and it exposed far more than engineering flaws. While the storm affected rich and poor alike, the wealthy evacuated while thousands of poor people remained stuck in town.

Even as Katrina was still destroying New Orleans, the blame game had begun. The hurricane was said to be God's wrath for any number of sins. God was punishing the vice industry of New Orleans (never mind that New Orleans' riches came from tourists). God was judging President Bush's refusal to join the Kyoto Protocol on climate change. God was judging the practice of slavery in U.S. history. Actual victims of the disaster were hardly real people; they were merely evidence.

Into the middle of the war of words strode Jesse Jackson. He had made a career of showing up at the right times to denounce some injustice or another. I for one thought I knew what he was going to say before he opened his mouth—I expected him to try to humiliate the Republican Party, or at least George W. Bush.

Which is why I was so surprised and chastened when the Reverend Jackson said nothing of the sort. Instead he invited a nation to compassion. "The people in this country have a high tolerance for viewing black pain," Jackson said. There is real suffering on the other side of your television set. Stop *viewing* it, and start *feeling* it.

He was not playing a political game. As a pastor, he was prodding the nation into a moment of spiritual decision.

Jackson's appeal to compassion invited us to engage the suffering occurring before our eyes. The beloved community is a suffering community. By the power of Christ's love, the church can drink deeply from the cup of human misery without needing to concern itself with self-preservation. By inviting the American people to feel black suffering, Jackson was inviting us to live like the church. Unfortunately, compassion hurts, and cool doesn't. Cool offered an alternative to people who were scared to let themselves feel compassion—or any other feeling.

Insensitivity to the reality of human suffering is cool.

As long as we're preoccupied with being cool, we can't feel other people's pain. We can only view it. That's why we began our affair with cool in the first place: so life wouldn't hurt us so much. Insensitivity to the reality of human suffering is cool.

A TALE OF TWO KINGS

In the summer of 1954, America was on the verge of two of its most important social transformations. A young pastor, Martin Luther King Jr., graduated from seminary and spent the summer negotiating a salary with a middle-class church in Alabama. Three hundred miles to the west a young delivery truck driver, Elvis Presley, stepped into a small record studio hoping for a job as a singer. King's leadership of a local bus boycott would catalyze the civil rights movement. Presley would bring cool rebellion to a generation of bored young whites.

In 1955 Martin Luther King Jr. was thrust into the leadership of the Montgomery bus boycott because he was the new pastor in town. As the boycott progressed, however, he became less comfortable with his role. Death threats were coming in, and he was terrified. In the middle of the night on January 27, 1956, King couldn't sleep. So he went into the kitchen, made some coffee and began listening to God. He recounts what happened next:

> I heard the voice of Jesus saying still to fight on. He promised never to leave me, never to leave me alone. No never alone. No never alone. He promised never to leave me, never to leave me alone.

At that moment, King went from being a reluctant leader to being a prophet. If he was leading a rebellion, it was not a private rebellion. It was action coming out of a relationship. Jesus was never going to leave King alone. Accordingly, it was never again about King himself. He made the daring attempt to cast the civil rights movement in universal terms, to build a beloved community, a truly interracial church and society.

Meanwhile, Elvis Presley had started his career as a singer. His music was profoundly multiethnic, and would inspire successor bands like the Beatles, the Rolling Stones and the Animals to dig into black music for fresh ideas. But while Martin Luther King's mission was to create a multiracial society (believing that desegregation would solve racism), white rock and roll musicians did not pursue racial healing. White audiences knew that the source of their favorite music had come from black musicians but bought records by the white performers anyway. White musicians like Elvis appropriated black tunes and got rich while countless black musicians struggled in obscurity to put bread on the table.

Rock and roll was thought by its founders to be revolutionary and made promises of social transformation: the liberation of individuals from the various expectations (moral, career or otherwise) of the broader community. The genre quickly progressed far beyond Elvis Presley, rejecting authority altogether. By 1969, Elvis was stuck as a sideshow act in Las Vegas. He was not even invited to Woodstock, that era's epicenter of cool. Martin Luther King didn't even make it that far; he was shot dead the year before.

CHANGING COURSE

Perhaps unfairly, Elvis has become for many the personification of the lost opportunity of the late fifties. Elvis today is as much myth as historical figure, and the myth has two different versions: Saint Elvis, who liberated the (white) masses, and Thief Elvis, who stole black culture. Martin Luther King has become a mythical figure as well, turned into a nonthreatening teddy bear by the same institutions that felt most threatened by him in his lifetime.

In the spring of 1968 Dolphus Weary, a black student at a white Christian liberal arts college, overheard white students on campus celebrating Dr. King's murder.

> "These Christian kids were glad that Dr. King—my hero—had been shot. I wanted to run out there and confront them." Instead, he steeled his fury and laid prostrate on his bed. Finally, as the newscaster delivered the awful update—"Martin Luther King has died in a Memphis hospital."—Weary could hear the white voices down the hall let out a cheer.

The unwillingness of white Christians to move beyond viewing to feeling and entering into the suffering of the black community convinced the fledgling Black Power movement that King's message of Christian weakness was distasteful. Even before his assassination, King's movement, like the movement that started with Presley, took a radical turn and disowned its founder. Their contempt manifested as cool. The Black Power movement announced itself in the late sixties, initially with a message of full human dignity. Speaking to a largely white evangelical audience at InterVarsity's 1970 Urbana convention, Tom Skinner said:

For those of us who live in the black community, it was not the evangelical who came and taught us our worth and dignity as black men. It was not the Bible-believing fundamentalist who stood up and told us that black was beautiful. It was not the evangelical who preached to us that we should stand on our two feet and be men, be proud that black was beautiful and that God could work his life out through our redeemed blackness. Rather, it took Malcolm X, Stokely Carmichael, Rap Brown and the brothers to declare to us our dignity. God will not be without a witness.

Efforts by African American artists to reinforce King's reconciling message began to wane in the late 1960s and early 1970s. Soul singer Sam Cooke, participating in the African American literary tradition of "masking" (speaking with double meanings), had once appealed to his white audience to look beyond color and cultural history to find a future together:

Don't know much about history
Don't know much biology . . .
But I do know that I love you
And I know that if you love me too
What a wonderful world this would be.

But mainstream America ate up the music and never bothered to ask if there was a message. So the black power movement stressed black self-determination, in culture as well as politics, and gloried in masculine and partriarchal power, as well as white fear. The band Parliament took a different tack from Sam Cooke in their song "Chocolate City." "Gainin' on Ya!"—the song's haunting refrain—was a far cry from an invitation to reconciliation. It was a proclamation of aggression.

A subset of the movement was Black Arts, which explicitly called for "a radical reordering of the western cultural aesthetic. It pro-pose[d] a separate symbolism, mythology, critique, and iconology." Ten years later, that vision became reality with hip hop. Todd Boyd says, "Hip hop has rejected and now replaced the pious, sanctimo-nious nature of civil rights as the defining moment of Blackness. In turn, it offers new ways of seeing and understanding what it means to be Black at this pivotal moment in history."

Drawing on West African musical origins, hip hop arose in the 1970s out of block parties in the slums of the Bronx. Disc jockeys at these parties would bring two copies of their favorite disco and funk records, and hook up two turntables to the stereo system. They could play an extended version of the song's instrumental break by switch-ing back and forth from one turntable to the other.

During these instrumental breaks, the crowd might begin to lose interest. The DJ would speak into the microphone over the records, encouraging the crowd to keep it together. These early "raps" were mainly exhortations for the best dancers to find their way to the front to show off their moves and dance each other off stage. Break dancers, or B-Boys as they came to be called, were not all out to promote black power. They were just kids from the neighbor-hood, trying to be cool.

You don't wear shades because the future's so bright. You wear shades because your eyes betray you.

Hip hop carefully maintains its boundaries through the cultural vehicle of shame, specifically the threat of uncool. Parliament made the explicit connection, in their song "P.Funk," between cool-ness and black power: "You got to wear your sun-glasses. So you can feel cool." You don't wear shades because the future's so bright. You wear shades because your eyes betray you. Parliament, who took ornamentation and smooth dance moves to a higher level, wanted to be looked at, but didn't really want to be known.

VANILLA ICE AND THE ONGOING STRUGGLE

In 1990 rappers Public Enemy conflated Elvis with "the powers that be" in their song "Fight the Power." The same year, a white rapper named Vanilla Ice topped the charts with his song "Ice Ice Baby." He told of growing up in an all-black environment (and was subsequently outed as a liar). In the public discourse, Vanilla Ice eventually became a fresh symbol of white theft of black culture; now everyone had the opportunity to respond to Elvis all over again.

Meanwhile, hip hop was developing a taste for thugs. In a convoluted and conflicted line of reasoning, some black Muslims in the 1960s began touting all things Asian as the source of power and secret knowledge. Asia was "deep" and accordingly had deeper criminals. *Thugees*—murderous gangs in India associated with *Kali,* the Black Goddess (the Hindu goddess of death and the namesake of the city Calcutta)—were known for roaming the Indian countryside after religious festivals, terrorizing the populace and frustrating British attempts to control them. (A fictional revival of the *thugee* cult was featured in the 1984 film *Indiana Jones and the Temple of Doom.*) Thug imagery and motifs began showing up in edgier hip hop records, like the Wu-Tang Clan's influential 1999 CD *Wu-Tang Forever.*

One white boy from California so took to the thug concept that he adapted an online black persona, posting on thug websites about Islam, mystical power and anti-American violence. "John Doe," as he called himself, eventually tired of talking about the revolution, left the country and made for the Middle East. Now calling himself Abdul Hamid, and whose passport read John Walker Lindh, ended up fighting for the Mujahiddeen in Afghanistan before being arrested by American soldiers in 2001.

HOW TO RENT A NEGRO

Lindh's story leads us to a major question: why do white Americans and Europeans seek out blackness, or *négritude,* as the French call it?

Cleary this white quest has not always come out of a desire for inter-racial relationships. Elvis Presley's success derives in part from the sizeable market in white America for a variation on cool that didn't require getting to know real-life African Americans.

White fascination with blackness ranges from "Jungle Fever" (lust) to exoticism to vague feelings of guilt for slavery. In *How to Rent a Negro*, Damali Ayo sarcastically suggests black people should start charging whites for the use of their blackness, noting that vouching for a white person's coolness in front of other whites could be worth a lot of money. This money would supposedly compensate both for the daily accommodations African Americans make for white hypersensitivities, and for the financial loss suffered by a felt cultural theft in process since the dawn of recorded music.

As Bakari Kitwana notes in *Why White Kids Love Hip Hop*, white fans of hip hop do not necessarily want to be black. Rather, they usually resonate with the message and long for the perceived community of the hip hop world. The overriding African American chorus about cultural theft is not so much about the money as it is about respect. It is thus crucial to distinguish between loving cool *négritude* and loving real black human beings.

Twelve years after Vanilla Ice, white rapper Eminem acknowledged the burden of history in his song "Without Me": "I am the worst thing since Elvis Presley/To do Black music so selfishly/And use it to get myself wealthy." In the song "White America," from the same 2002 album, he said: "Look at my sales, let's do the math, if I was black, I would've sold half." Eminem understood the racial inequalities in the system. He and other white rappers work overtime to combat the threat of being shamed as cultural thieves.

MISSED OPPORTUNITIES

For a full generation now, hip hop's advocates have waxed eloquent about their music's revolutionary potential, but to build a movement with real power requires the sort of stamina and dedication we saw in the early civil rights movement—and most kinds of stamina are not cool. The title of Eldridge Cleaver's 1968 manifesto for the Black Power movement, *Soul on Ice*, lets us in on this worldview: real power is about a cool, even frozen heart. To this day *Soul on Ice* remains a primary textbook in college classes, even though Cleaver himself came to retract most of his views. (His 1978 memoir of healing from hatred, *Soul on Fire*, has sold far fewer copies.)

Rejecting the machismo in much of today's hip-hop, feminist bell hooks comments that "black men dealing with their childhoods is the revolutionary act." To extend hooks's observation beyond black men: as long as we train ourselves not to be affected by the suffering in the world; as long as our hearts remain insensitive to those around us; as long as we worry about our cool more than about the well-being of the hurting, lost and downtrodden, we will remain spiritually impotent—commercial success notwithstanding. Black power and hip hop aren't the problem; cool is the problem.

Over the nine years that I've been a member of a historically, and still predominantly African American church, I've seen a curious parade of whites pass through. Many stay for only a few months before getting disillusioned and moving on. For some of these passersby, the trouble with my church is that most members care more about honoring God, and taking the gospel to the world, than they do about being cool.

I can tell within seconds which ones are here for church, which ones are here on an anthropological expedition, and which ones are here to *catch them some cool*. Some talk with a hip hop accent, even to adults; some mug with the pastor and seek acceptance from church members. They avoid talking to me; as a white person in a black church, I am not what they came here for.

It's kind of embarrassing, actually, because they're not fooling anyone. Generation after generation of African Americans have seen whites make the same mistakes and offend in the same ways. In 1927, Rudolph Fisher wrote an influential essay entitled "The Caucasian Storms Harlem," taking a look at the white patrons of jazz clubs in New York's largest black neighborhood.

> Is this [white] interest akin to that of the Virginians on the ve-
> randa of a plantation's big-house—sitting genuinely spellbound
> as they hear the lugubrious strains floating up from the Negro
> quarters? Is it akin to that of the African explorer, Stanley, leav-
> ing a village far behind, but halting in spite of himself to catch
> the boom of its distant drum?

Today, white America knows scarcely more about the souls of black folks than eighty years ago, but we know infinitely more dance moves. And we wonder that people talk about cultural theft!

EXPORTING COOL

But is it still theft if it's a brand new cultural product? Today's cool has acquired a truly global existence. It is one of America's most influential inventions, but it no longer remains in its inventors' control. Americans have displayed a mixture of bewilderment and alarm at the popularity, across much of the Muslim world, of Osama Bin Laden t-shirts and posters. "Are these people terrorist sympathizers?" we ask. To an extent, the answer is yes, but not for the reasons Americans fear. For many people around the world, Bin Laden is today's Ché Guevara, a man unafraid of provoking what country singer Toby Keith has called "The Angry American."

Los Angeles, Mexico City and Prague all burned with unrest in 1968, but nowhere did protesters come closest to overthrowing a government than in France. In 1968, student insurrections against rigidity in the education system shook French society. For a few short days, as an entire nation held its breath, students engaged the police in pitched street battles. Students tore up Paris' cobblestones for ammunition, while police brutality, caught on camera, turned the general population against the government. But the revolution never came. The riots ended when school got out for summer, and students took off for the beach.

The revolution went nowhere because it had nowhere to go. Just like countless student protesters since then, the French students were bored in the first place and idealistic later. They had watched Californian anti-war protests on television. Cool makes for great street performance, but doesn't lend itself well to serious activism.

Just as whites once appropriated black cool without any love for black people, so today's global cool has little to do with love for America. Italian-born German rapper Afrob addresses Germany's immigration policies. *Time* magazine's 2005 profile of the French underground introduced readers to young men "in their hooded sweatshirts [going] by rapper tags—Spion, El Pach, Benou and K-Soc." Looking at the Asian scene, Todd Boyd describes "Japanese youth bouncing to the phattest track in Tokyo's Roppongi district." Indian acts have brought traditional percussion to hip hop, and a real and vital energy. Meanwhile back in the old continent of Africa, Daara J sings bilingually in Wolof and French, blending traditional griot music with messages about hip hop coming home: "Hip hop was born in Africa [and] went around the world to come back to Africa, like a boomerang."

> Cool makes for great street performance, but doesn't lend itself well to serious activism.

So, like a boomerang, America has given itself over to cool, only to ultimately lose its cool. From cities to country clubs; from sex to religion to music, cool's omnipresence is a constant reminder of America's unfulfilled potential. Even as the world has taken what it wants and moved on, America is alone and isolated, like Elvis Presley at the end of his life: cool without heart, hiding our hurt behind a cool façade but without a joy in the world. Misery is more prominent in American culture than ever before. We all want to be cool, and we are willing to sacrifice family to get it. In our attempts to exclude outsiders and assert our individuality, we lose touch with the beloved community, and with it our joy.

JOY IS FOR US

In his short letter to the Philippians, Paul uses the words *joy* or *rejoice* thirteen times. Joy is a command. Joy is something we choose. And since joy is an act of the will, it is more meaningful than the randomness of happiness or luck.

Joy is for the children of God. Joy is a communal fruit. It is the soap that washes away cool's addictive toxins. Joy removes from our hearts the need for self-protection, and in the process gives us much greater insight into reality than cool.

Human nature and spiritual nature operate from radically different starting points. Cool is like a layer of callus on our hands: cool protects us from pain. But God cares too much about reconciled relationships, between himself and the world, and between human beings created in his image, to worry about moments of discomfort. God's love coaxes our terrified hearts out into the open. "Is it safe?" we ask. "No," God replies. "If you let me in, you will experience all the pain you can imagine right now. More even. You'll get to feel the same pain I do every day when I look at my world. And you'll get to feel the same love."

Christian love in community is the real deal, more authentic than cool will ever know. When Christians love people like Jesus did, cold and wounded hearts get healed and generations of hatred can wash away. This is supernatural work. It is more radical than a mere rejection of cool. For a lonely and suffering world, God's love—the church's love—is good news indeed.

Unfortunately, we are too busy trying to be cool to notice.

4

FAITH-BASED COOL

Rebellion, Individualism and Assimilation

"Jesus is just the best trip, man." "Jesus is a rebel." "My goal is to destroy Christianity." Welcome to the Orwellian world of cool Christianity, where the most powerful and beautiful treasures in the world get coated with cheap paint. Cool Christianity: we are tinsel town.

At first glance, as we look over the history of the church's various cool sales jingles, we want to cringe with embarrassment. *Did we really say that?* The point of most of these churchy sales pitches is partly to impute a breath of fresh air into inbred faith, and partly to cool up faith. That is not in itself a bad thing. It is a good idea for Christians to continually take a new look at Jesus. It is furthermore important for each generation of young Christians to encounter Christ in the context of the changing world around them. But Christians have been doing that for two thousand years. Sometimes in our innovations we've cooked up very bad ideas. In the first century, the Corinthians twisted the Christian concept of love to come up with a free-love theology, a development Paul found dangerous and destructive to the church. And within living memory, American Christians have actively taught that racial segregation is God's desire for the church.

Similarly, most cool Jesuses are distortions of the gospel. Whenever in our eagerness for relevance we begin to create heresies, anti-

As long as our faith is cool, we will remain incapable of the kind of love that Jesus demands of us.

social dead-ends or unsustainable schisms, we need to courageously step away from them. Neither private rebellion, nor living for the moment, has any place in our communal and eternity-minded faith. As long as we try to infuse our faith with a dose of cool, we will end up with a faith obsessed with rebellion rather than repentance. We will always be in danger of becoming the very hell we are vying against. As long as our faith is cool, we will remain incapable of the kind of love that Jesus demands of us.

THE FEEDBACK LOOP

Jesus was explicit about the cost of discipleship: "Whoever wants to be my disciple must deny themselves and take up their cross and follow me. For whoever wants to save their life will lose it, but whoever loses their life for me and for the gospel will save it" (Mark 8:34-35); "Those of you who do not give up everything you have cannot be my disciples" (Luke 14:33); "You do not belong to the world, but I have chosen you out of the world. That is why the world hates you." (John 15:19).

Jesus never glamorized the world's hatred. He viewed it instead as a simple matter of fact. But in an amazing confusion of cause and effect, cool Christianity glories in the world's contempt. It is as if we think God's favor comes from our offending the world. And then we busy ourselves trying to reinvent cool within the confines of our subculture—separating ourselves from the world while judging ourselves by the world's standards. We are cool, we declare, but in a Christian way.

Douglas Rushkoff has observed a phenomenon he calls a "feedback loop" between culture and marketing, whereby people internalize the messages of advertising to such an extent that they try to reshape their lives in the advertisements' image. "It becomes impossible to tell," he observes, "which came first—the anger or the marketing of the anger."

Cool Christianity indulges in a similar feedback loop. Cool Christianity projects a Christian variant of cool that is identical to—but for the most part flies under the radar of—cool's cultural centers. Accordingly, most cool Christianity is an internal performance for our own consumption. We create it to feel better about ourselves.

Cool Christianity assumes an insider position under the watchful eye of outsiders. The performance of cool Christianity serves both to make the insider feel cool and to invite outsiders in. In the process, however, the insiders experience schism after schism, as cool Christianity confronts and rejects its forebears. Ultimately, what's left looks hollow to outsiders—a pale imitation of the cool they've come to love.

Most cool Christianity is an internal performance for our own consumption. We create it to feel better about ourselves.

Ten years ago, I visited a prominent evangelical college that I was considering for higher education. The weekend included several student life events, meant to give me a taste of the college's social life. On Saturday night, I experienced a parade of cool feedback, at a rock show on campus disingenuously called the "Wagasm." As the band tortured aggressive sound out of their guitars with the help of Wa-wa distortion pedals, students bopped their heads in a timid attempt to challenge the school's no-dancing policy. Throughout the weekend, in fact, students repeatedly complained to me about the school's restrictive moral code. Their cool couldn't be imprisoned by any no-dancing rules. They were *hip* in the original African sense of the word—they saw further than the unenlightened school administrators.

It all seemed a little silly to me. These kids were well aware of the school's moral restrictions when they enrolled. If adherence was such a hardship, hundreds of other colleges were available. I chose to attend my local state school, UW-Madison, instead. I decided that it would be easier to remain a healthy Christian at a stridently irreligious institution than at a Christian college.

I still believe that. But at Wisconsin I encountered the same feedback loop: Christian concern for a cool reputation. Going out of their way to disassociate from "intolerant" conservatives, students involved in evangelism through various campus ministries explicitly disavowed "religion" in favor of the much hipper "spirituality." Since Madison was one of the nation's most politically active campuses, Christian students framed their evangelism in activist language. "If you really want to overthrow corporate America, try Christianity."

FREE-MARKET FAITH

Meanwhile, corporate America was taking a good look at Christian consumers and seeing plenty of money to be made from the feedback loop. Christians are willing to part with large amounts of cash for access to Christian cool. Today some of the biggest and coolest Christian bands are produced by mainstream corporate concerns Time Warner, Sony and Universal.

There's nothing wrong with Christian music being integrated into the global market. God is glorified by excellence in our craftsmanship. Lots of top-quality Christian music produced by multinational corporations will be present in heaven. Still, the church has been seduced by cool. Ever since cool called the church ugly, we've been ingratiating ourselves at cool's feet. Like Adam and Eve, we are ashamed of our nakedness—ashamed of the beauty we have in Christ. The apostle Paul confronted a similar fear among the Christians in Ephesus:

> And God raised us up with Christ and seated us with him in the heavenly realms in Christ Jesus. . . . For we are God's workmanship, created in Christ Jesus to do good works, which God prepared in advance for us to do. (Ephesians 2:6, 10)

Do we dare reject cool at the moment of glory? It's a costly choice: if we even cast a moment's glance over our shoulders, if we even shudder with doubt, the gods of hip will turn us to salt. If we dump cool, cool will never take us back.

So cool demands a steep tax: spiritual lameness. Sin, repentance and modesty are inappropriate topics of discussion among cool circles. Americans sit atop a four-hundred year legacy of religious freedom and diversity; whereas traditional societies (such as those in the Middle East) see religion as consensual and authoritative, faith in North America has almost always operated within the open market. Indeed, the freedom to change religions has become fundamental not just in law but in the spiritual thinking of American faith. After a pointless thirty-year long religious war destroyed much of Europe, the old world disgorged **If we dump cool, cool will never take us back.** hordes of cults, sects and schismatics onto American shores. Meanwhile, when Roger Williams, the new world's first Baptist, was expelled from Massachusetts, he moved down the road and established his own church in his own colony, Rhode Island. Over the next century and a half, countless church disputes resolved themselves in this manner. By the 1780s, America was so religiously diverse that it had become impossible to preface a constitution for the new nation with the words "We the people," without subsequently enshrining extensive religious freedom.

When a church in Georgia wanted to reach disaffected punks and skaters, they decided to preach a message of contempt for the church. With their intentionally shocking "Religion Kills" campaign, they pronounced a radical gulf between themselves and the mainstream church. These well-intentioned evangelists were angered by the larger church, and with good reason: the church provided no home for these skater-punks. But while it's fine and good to give to the disenfranchised a Jesus who looks like them, the method of this church's outreach prized acceptance from people outside the church over reconciliation and communion with the (embarrassingly) conventional church.

IN SEARCH OF THE TRUTH

It may be broken, divisive and at times fully implicated in atrocities, but God still chooses to work out his grace through the church. If cool Christians wish to send "the church" to hell, and promote some anti-structure instead, we had better be sure of what we're doing. Whatever distortions there are in evangelistic campaigns shape the kind of Christians that grow out of them. If non-Christians join the church to rebel against the devil, they haven't really centered their faith in Christ. If Jesus is the "best trip," sober Christian discipleship isn't attractive.

Was Jesus really a rebel? Yes, but Jesus didn't rage against some abstract machine; he called people to an old way, the way revealed in the prophets. The way of doing life that Jesus championed had never been done because it had always been resisted. Jesus rocked the boat, and defied the status quo, modeling courageous resistance of the prevailing winds. But in our contemporary culture, rebellion is considered a good in its own right—and a thrilling one at that. We're out to transgress. But we don't really have any agenda beyond rebellion itself. Was Jesus really a rebel? Sure. But our version of rebellion is a shallow impression.

Marketing cool Christianity is a dangerous proposition. Jesus-as-rebel is a gospel that misleads non-Christians, stunts the maturity of new believers and undermines the centrality of the church. Conversion, stripped of its transformative power, is often today scarcely more than tribal defection.

In one of the most personal reports I've ever seen on cool Christianity, *Gentlemen's Quarterly* writer John Jeremiah Sullivan attends a large-scale Christian music festival in the Pennsylvania countryside, where his cool and superior attitude gets neatly blown away by the self-contented joy of the three backwoods West Virginia boys with whom he spent most of his weekend.

> Statistically speaking, my bout with Evangelicalism was probably unremarkable. For white Americans with my socioeconomic background (middle to upper-middle class), it's an experience commonly linked to one's teens and moved beyond before one reaches 20.

Sullivan understood the purpose of Christian cool to keep the kids going through their "Jesus phase," as he calls it, from leaving the church. But through long nights around the campfire with three West Virginia boys, eating frogs they had speared in a nearby creek, Sullivan got a glimpse past the Christian cool of mainstream evangelicalism.

Sullivan's new acquaintances told him he could call them crazy if he wanted, but asked him to mention that they loved the Lord. The Christian-rock bands didn't do it for him. The us-against-the-world paranoia steeping much of the festival played into his stereotypes. Cool Christianity smelled like old fish. But the authenticity and joy of three young men thoroughly disarmed him, and forced him to reckon with his own decision to walk away from the faith of his youth.

We will live a healthier and more compelling faith when we get over our cool and open our hearts and homes to the lost, hurting, lonely and yes, even the arrogant and cool.

INWARD REBELLION

Cool is all about private rebellion, and so cool needs something to rebel against. And its favorite targets are whatever authorities impinge on individualism and privacy. And which authority makes bigger claims upon the privacy of the individual: the church or the world? It's not even close.

It is only a small step from rebellion against the world, to rebellion against the church. Once the church appropriated cool as a device for *outreach,* cool began to exploit fertile territory *within* faith. This rebellion typically manifests as generational hostility, which is to say, generational hostility between young adults and baby boomers. It's at times a veiled threat. "Megachurch," for many young urban Christians, is less a real form of church than an aesthetic slander without much spiritual content. We think gentle colors and sweet music is ignorant. We accuse megachurches of watering down the faith. Here's what one urban pastor in Michigan told the *New York Times:*

> The deity-free "church lite" of the megachurches—that's the last thing these people want. They want to talk about God. It's hardcore, not in a fire and brimstone way, but it has to be raw, real.

Does "raw" have any more content than "deity-free 'church lite'"? The distinction is aesthetic and semantic. God's church, on the other hand, is organic. The church, created in God's three-in-one image, is communal. The church is the church—the beloved community—no matter how conventional, hokey, Republican or boomeresque. Is the cool church any more loving than the world we profess to care for? Or do we just want to kill our fathers?

REDEEMING REBELLION

When Christians enter the arena of rebellion, we are playing with hellfire. That being said, rebellion can be a tool for the good, because rebellion can be used to provoke justice, or to frustrate injustice.

Not all rebellion is un-Christian, of course. In God's economy, rebellion—humbly stewarded—can be a valuable tool for justice and mercy. Sometimes badness must be resisted. The problem is that rebellion stirs such passion in our hearts. We can no more flee rebellion, with all its seductive power, than we can flee our sexuality or other powerful elements of our souls. Fleeing rebellion is a form of cowardice, because sometimes, as Christians, we need to rebel.

In our cool-drenched culture, we have a hard time imagining what authentic Christian rebels might look like. But they exist! One such rebel was simultaneously one of the most talented and least cool humans to ever set the English language to pen: an Englishman by the name of John Milton.

Born in 1608, Milton was an ambitious young man, who set out to become his generation's most famous poet. But God had other plans. After publishing a few unremarkable poems, Milton began to look around him. Was his poetry relevant at all? The Holy Spirit began to impress on him the needs of the suffering and persecuted church in his own country. Archbishop Laud was determined to violently rid England of non-Anglicans, while Milton sat in the lap of luxury writing poetry.

So he opened his heart to God's calling, making himself available no matter what God asked of him. And God asked him for his career and reputation. Milton agonized, but ultimately submitted. Henceforth, he would no longer write for his own fame. He would use his gifts for the cause of justice.

The cause of justice led Milton into a heap of trouble. His pamphlets in favor of religious freedom and freedom of the press infuriated the Anglican hierarchy, but helped bring the population to a boiling point. Milton came to believe that even kings needed to submit to justice, and he joined a rebel elite that overthrew Charles I, tried him and executed him in 1649.

Milton continued to advocate for religious liberty in England, producing pamphlet after pamphlet (the documentary short of its day). By this point, Milton was England's most famous agitator, and hardly anyone remembered that he had started off as a poet.

Like countless other revolutionaries, Milton then watched the rebel movement self-destruct. The 1650s—when Britain had no king—turned out to be one of the bloodiest decades in British history. Parliament's chosen "Lord Protector," Oliver Cromwell, launched a genocide in Ireland, butchering countless citizens for the dual crimes of Catholicism and loyalty to Charles. But the rebels overextended, and in 1660, the monarchy was restored in Britain. The new king, Charles II, issued a general amnesty to most 1649 rebels, and Milton only made the cut by the skin of his teeth.

As he grew old, Milton took stock of his career. His was a mixed record: England now had a degree of religious freedom. But he had seen how merely taking out the oppressor does not get to the root of the problem. Without God's grace, human sin would always destroy any utopia. Authority itself wasn't the problem—evil was.

And so, in the winter of his life, blind and disappointed, Milton was released by God to pursue his first love. He would once again be free to write, but this time for God's glory, "to justify the ways of God to men," Milton said. He could no longer see well enough to write, so his daughter transcribed as he dictated what is arguably the finest single piece of literature in the English language: 1667's *Paradise Lost*.

After a lifetime in the pursuit of justice, John Milton was bent on understanding Satan's character. *Paradise Lost* tells the story of Adam and Eve's fall, mainly from the perspective of Satan, the originator of rebellion. Milton saw Adam and Eve's fall as merely a subset of Satan's previous war with God.

As Satan departs hell for the purpose of destroying Adam and Eve, he explains his motivation to his fellow fallen angels: "Better to reign in hell, than serve in heav'n" (book 1, line 263). Satan is, of course, fooling no one except himself, but he will at least try to bring Adam and Eve down with him out of spite.

Satan further claims to be able to make a heaven out of hell (1:255). This notion has a remarkably contemporary ring to it, but should we believe him? He is Satan, after all, the father of all lies. Satan is his own first victim: he can't tell truth from lies anymore, so warped is his perception of reality.

Paradise is lost to Adam and Eve because Satan persuaded them to rebel against the only authority they had ever known. But they quickly discover that none of the gains they'd hoped for materialize. Indeed, they discover, in their rebellion they had thrown away every freedom worth having. Even their lovemaking—graphically related in Book 4—is less satisfactory than before: Adam seizes Eve, and each takes from each other (9:1037-1042). Mutual giving has been replaced with self-righteousness and isolation.

> Thus they in mutual accusation spent
> The fruitless hours, but neither self-condemning,
> And of their vain contest appeared no end. (9:1187-1189)

Paradise Lost has a way of getting under people's skin precisely because Milton demands that we see the entire universe—from our inter-human quarreling, to our sexuality, to nature itself—as residing under God's authority. Our whole lives are to be lived in submission to God and to whatever authorities he anoints; and in strife with whatever puts itself above God. Milton thunders with a deeply threatening beauty and authority that shakes our individualism to the core.

From a Christian perspective, bad authority is bad, and good authority is good.

From a Christian perspective, bad authority is bad, and good authority is good. The former should be resisted, and the latter should be reverently acknowledged. But where we have taken too many cues from our surrounding culture, we consider "good authority" to be a contradiction. When conflict arises, rather than sit down and resolve our differences, we bolt for greener pastures. We leave churches over worship styles, and there are countless believers with no formal relationships with any local church. As Christians, our starting point in conflict needs to be a willingness to turn the other cheek. When we can overcome our disagreements, the church can become the beloved community, the source of true power for social change.

LOVING JUSTICE AND MERCY

An amazing transformation is taking place in the American church, before our very eyes: after nearly a century of spirituality with little emphasis on social concern, evangelicals in large numbers are beginning to grasp the gospel's concern for justice. Multiple agencies and movements are cropping up, Christian student groups are rediscovering activism, and justice and mercy are going mainstream.

Evangelicals have a wonderful quality when it comes to change: if evangelicals can be convinced that the Bible teaches such-and-such, they'll make genuine efforts to change. In an interview with *Christianity Today*, one pastor described a typical evangelical experience: he began to

> reexamine Scripture with "new eyes." What he found humbled him. "I found those 2,000 verses on the poor. How did I miss that? I went to Bible College, two seminaries, and I got a doctorate. How did I miss God's compassion for the poor?"

Of course, not only have those 2,000 verses been there all along, but "the church" has never stopped teaching them. African American Christians have over a century's unbroken record of teaching on poverty and injustice. Many mainline churches would never let someone get a doctorate without a solid grasp on biblical compassion. In the developing world, where pastors deal with disease and oppression on a daily basis, the church has been eating theological meat for decades, if not centuries.

There's no need to reinvent the wheel. It's not cool to admit a mistake, and it's humbling to visit the "dead" church across town, only to find bookshelves crammed with biblically sound teachings on justice. But the church has the authority and mission to announce the kingdom of God. Rebellion can be redeemed once we stop asserting our individuality or trying to make a name for ourselves.

The church's power comes from the cross. As long as we cling to cool, whether in our hearts or in our churches, we will lack the moral strength to pick up our cross and follow Jesus to the grave. Cool is a nasty little habit, but once we shake it, we'll begin to experience new life in our hearts. Let us now explore that new life.

PART TWO

The Stuff of Real Life

5

THE TAO OF JESUS

Faith, Hope and Love Ain't Cool

The drunken sobs coming from the stairwell still haunt my memories of Witte Hall, my dormitory at the University of Wisconsin. There's nothing like alcohol to expose people's real feelings; that's one of the reasons they binge in the first place. But drunk or not, this young woman's tears were still real, and for all of us who heard them, her cries were the sound of misery. She had gone off to some party somewhere with several other women from my floor, a party where she probably didn't know anyone. She had obviously buried her anxieties in alcohol. But the booze didn't make it any better, and somebody needed to help. After some discussion, a group of us standing around in the hallway fetched some of her friends to take care of her. They talked to her for a while and brought her inside. Was that the right choice? I still wonder if there was something bigger I could have done. What does compassion look like when people are hurting like that? Does compassion stop her from getting drunk in the first place? Does compassion merely put out the fires?

One time I found a kid on the floor of the bathroom, naked from the waist down. He had gotten nauseated, but instead of leaning over the toilet to vomit, had pulled down his pants and sat down. Then he had leaned forward and puked into his pants. After removing his pants, he had made for the door before falling asleep on the tile floor. I got a washrag and a towel, cleaned him up and covered his privates, and put him to sleep on my couch (on his side of course—they teach you at freshman orientation how to keep drunks from drowning in their own vomit). He didn't feel very cool when he sobered up, and he was right: cool hadn't followed him home, cool had stayed at the party on Orchard Street.

Orchard Street parties were beer parties, and they all followed a similar liturgy. People warmed up on Schlitz or some other cheap swill back in the dorm. When enough pilgrims had assembled to guarantee everyone's anonymity, the gaggle would descend to the street and wend its way to the party. Freshmen rarely knew where they were going, or who was hosting. Somebody knew somebody from high school, and everybody was invited. Bring five dollars to buy a cup.

It was a new semester and the kids were off to glory in the freedom of college, the fun of dancing and singing, and the glamour of gendered tension. For the most part, I suppose, it was innocent fun. But why did so many parties end like this? Someone always got hurt. Unwanted intercourse was a normal event after these parties. Women were getting violated at parties up and down Orchard Street. I once saw a young man slam a woman against the wall and start tearing at the cloth covering her breasts, while she groggily looked up at him. After checking to see that her friends were aware of what was happening, I walked out. I had had enough.

Years later I continue to question that choice. Should I have beaten the tar out of the punk who was groping her? Would a mere shove have done the trick? Should I have played chaperone and interrupted? What is the right thing to do in a situation like that? Paralyzed by the magnitude of the sin, I let this one crawl off into my forest of questions, memories and regrets.

Earlier that same day I'd seen some gymnastics on TV. It had been a religious experience for me; in the middle of an immaculate uneven parallel bars routine, I had felt God's majesty show through the screen. How could such human perfection be so closely related to the degradation I saw later that night? Worse yet, since gymnasts are mostly teenagers themselves, *in a few years this athlete could be that girl being attacked.* I couldn't take it, so I walked around the corner, got myself a donut and went home.

As bad as these parties are, nothing at Wisconsin could compare to Zurich's Platzspitz Park. In a misguided attempt to contain heroin usage and the spread of HIV, for a time the Swiss government allowed consumption on a little downtown spit of land between two rivers. Human misery mushroomed throughout the city during the years of containment.

Heroin is hell. The look in an addict's eyes is ghastly. Their humanity is still present, but every shred of dignity is gone. Depending on how close they are to their next fix, or how malnourished they are, they stutter and shake.

My friends and I ventured down to Platzspitz a few times, to buy cheap CDs from addicts. The best bargains can be coaxed out of the worst off. If they're only a few franks short of their next fix, or if they're overdue, it's a buyer's market. Give them their cash, and they drop everything to hurry over to the Lebanese dude with shades—the only other human-looking creature in the park. In a few minutes, this mother's child, this beautiful image of God, will be lying comatose on the ground as the onsite paramedics tip the corpse on its side, so the poor critter can't drown on its own vomit.

To this day I feel strongly wherever I encounter heroin, whether in addicts who come to church or in discarded needles behind night clubs or even on the silver screen. Very few drug movies do justice to heroin. Even as they graphically portray overdoses, Oliver Stone (*The Doors*) and Quentin Tarantino (*Pulp Fiction*) manage to make heroin seem fairly enlightened. *Trainspotting* makes a valiant attempt, by focusing on withdrawal. Better yet is *Crash*, which depicts the relational degradation fixed by a mother's addiction. I truly believe heroin is an evil from the pit of hell itself. I can't take heroin jokes. I can't go to pawn shops; looking at guitars, power tools and stereos, for the most part sold in a financial pinch, reminds me the time I looked hell in the eyes.

Of course, lives are getting destroyed all around us, every day, by all sorts of means. The poor are crushed by the rich, sometimes via anonymous devices like zoning codes and gerrymandered electoral districts. But destruction goes up the line. The hopes and dreams of the rich are perverted by the richer-yet. College students—the privileged ones of the world—come out of college with ridiculous piles of debt. Gender equality is becoming equality in oppression, as we are seeing surging rates of male eating disorders on the one hand and female pornography consumption on the other. Meanwhile society is turning children against their parents in the name of marketing, and each passing year sees children becoming more available to adults. People created with the capacity to know God and to create love are getting taken.

We need something bigger than cool. We need something authentic.

Cool may be less toxic than heroin or pornography, but it's toxic nonetheless. Cool makes us insensitive to bigger evils. Cool hobbles the church, turning us into a sick joke. We need something bigger than cool. We need something authentic.

DETOX

Detox is a special medical center for washing poisons out of our bodies. I've never been there, and hope never to. It's a deadly serious place, in every sense of the word. Detox is where you go when, unless you get immediate help, you're going to die.

A world going to hell needs Jesus even more desperately than an overdose victim needs detox. Does that sound dramatic enough? Death is all around us, devouring us, destroying us. Are we desperate enough to receive Christ? He might pump our stomachs. He might probe into corners of our hearts we ourselves are terrified to touch. He might begin to ask us for our treasured lies. Dare we let God take away our cool?

Human life is shockingly fragile and limited—shocking because human souls are oriented toward eternity. God made us for a bigger life than the one we've got. Cool and Christianity both concern themselves with the overwhelming limits to our lives; cool sees boundaries and reacts by transgressing them—it's cool to break the rules—while Christianity is more concerned with transcending the deadness. While we were dead in our transgressions, cool or otherwise, Christ came to give us the eternal life we are homesick for.

Lars Svendsen explains: "Transgression simply means exceeding or going beyond a limit. It can be moderate or radical, but it always takes place within the same plane. . . . Transcendence, on the other hand, implies more of a qualitative leap into something radically other." Transgression is the attitude a chained dog has toward his chain. "If I can only break this chain," the dog says, "I'll have what I want." That's transgression. Transcendence is the power to not be a dog anymore. The ultimate end of transgressing all possible boundaries is fragmentation. The goal of Christianity, on the other hand, is love with God and within his church, his beloved community, in this life. Christianity is thus at once immediate and transcendent—and it is way more profound than transgression, way deeper than cool.

With eternity-bound eyes, Christians see no glory in the morbid. There's nothing original about even the most revolting human concoctions. It's all been done before. The same depravity that systematically rapes the women of Darfur in the Sudan also plies women with booze on campus. The same poppy extract that knocks users into next week also defiles their humanity, eventually turning people created in God's image into pathetic and powerless addicts.

Transgression can be exciting in the short run, but it's ultimately boring, because the joy in transgression is primarily the joy of violating boundaries, not in actually enjoying what we find over there. And when all boundaries have been crossed, everything is equal and thus equally boring, numb and dead. But when God begins to heal us, when he begins to detoxify our minds from the lies we've believed, his transcendent reign appears. Life appears, and feeling. When everything we thought cool or liberating turns up empty or worse, a still, small voice whispers in the darkness: God is here, and he will not be silenced; his word is present in his church, the beloved community.

ANNOUNCING GOD'S REIGN

When we're at the very end, when our very souls are devastated along with our bodies and minds, when the questions we're most afraid to ask are the questions we most need to ask—"Why did you do that to me?" "Was it worth it?"—God is there. And he's not afraid of the mess. He's been there and has seen it from the bottom, looking up. And just as Jesus sent his disciples out into the villages, today he sends his church into every neighborhood, to "heal the sick who are there and tell them, 'the kingdom of God has come near to you'" (Luke 10:9).

So then what is this "kingdom"? It's not geographical, nor is it really a response to any power structures in the world. God is not out to contend with petty little empires on earth. The United States, China, Egypt, Wal-Mart, Microsoft or Manchester United: no dynasty is terribly impressive to God. But human suffering and sin are significant enough for God to act. He's out to create a beloved community—a people for himself, with whom he can join in fellowship forever.

John the Baptist was in prison, facing execution. After a career in courage, he finally got scared, and he sent his disciples to Jesus, asking if everything was true—if Jesus was really the Son of God. Jesus didn't give a straight affirmative reply. Instead he appealed to memory, telling John's disciples: "Go back and report to John what you hear and see: the blind receive sight, the lame walk, those who have leprosy are cleansed, the deaf hear, the dead are raised, and the good news is proclaimed to the poor" (Matthew 11:4-5).

God's reign was evidenced by healing, cleansing, restoring to life and proclaiming good news. Equally important, God's reign was evidenced among the outsiders: the blind, the lame, those with leprosy, the deaf, the dead and the poor.

Jesus told his prosecutors, "My kingdom is not of this world" (John 18:36). Jesus wasn't prepared to die for some revolution or other. He was however, planning on dying to establish his own kingdom. Allen Wakabayashi writes: "The kingdom of God is about *the dynamic of God's kingship being applied.*"

> God's reign descends in and through Jesus and is applied in a world that is not yet fully under his authority. Sicknesses are healed, demons are banished, sins are forgiven and people are assured of God's love for them. Wherever God's kingdom comes, his kingship comes, his kingship is applied and the evil of darkness is banished.

God's reign is one counterintuitive inversion after another. When we live in the power of God's reign, we are strongest when we feel weakest. We are most secure when we feel most exposed. God's power is evidenced by reckless compassion for the sick, the hurting and those who haven't heard the good news. God sends us out into every neighborhood to announce his kingdom, and the amazing thing is that, when we go, we discover his kingdom already at work.

THE WAY OF JESUS

In the beginning was Tao. Tao was with God and Tao was God. . . . And Tao became flesh and lived among us. That's a roundabout rendering in English of John 1:1, 14, as it stands in the Chinese Bible. The Chinese word *Tao* is similar to the Greek word *logos*, which means "word," "underlying order" and more. For John's original audience, living in the context of a Hebrew faith crossing cultures into a Greek world, *logos* additionally referred to God's revelation to humankind and the means of God's salvation. John was explicitly identifying Jesus (*logos* who became flesh and lived among us) with the origins of the universe and the cosmic forces. The English word *word* is woefully inadequate.

Tao, on the other hand, works much better, although it has plenty of religious baggage of its own from traditional Chinese religions. Usually translated as "way" in English, *Tao* has been defined as the natural order of the universe, humanly uncontrollable power, the little thing that is bigger than the big things, and so on. Chinese philosophers have often tried to describe *Tao* with stories and analogies, like "Tao is the smallest root of a plant of grass, almost invisible. But it can shatter rocks and bring down a house." People have filled books trying to explain *Tao*, and often conclude by insisting that *Tao* can't be defined or known.

God's kingdom inverts our expectations because our expectations are wrong.

When God's kingdom inverts our expectations, it is not because the kingdom is opposed to our world. It's because our expectations are wrong. What we *want* is a *Tao* that subverts the powers that be, but that's not the *Tao* we *need*. We need a transcendent way.

Cool is about rebellion—transgressing boundaries, whether social, physical, sexual or political. Beloved community, in contrast, is transcendent. The beloved community doesn't set out to violate social boundaries *for the sake of violating them*. It connects us with the infinite *Tao* in a way that transgression never can.

As John 1:14 makes explicit, *Tao* is not just an abstraction: he has a name and has made himself known to us in the person of Jesus. Jesus announced a new way—a transcendent way, a way he called

"God's kingdom." The arrival of God's reign is a miracle: we couldn't understand the ways of God, so God became flesh and lived among us. Jesus' way is upside-down from our expectations. It has a playful quality to it. It is impossible to predict how God will next advance his reign. And God's reign is flat-out impossible to control and tame. God keeps us alert.

At the same time, there is a pattern to God's activity in the world: he works through love and community. From the beginning of time, God lived in perfect community—Father, Son, Spirit. The three-in-one God lived in perfect community, more perfect than whatever love we can imagine. At creation the three-in-one God said, "Let *us* make human beings in *our* image, in *our* likeness" (Genesis 1:26, emphasis added). God temporarily, but absolutely broke perfect community for the sake of human beings created in his image but now doomed to hell. That's what Jesus was experiencing when he cried out from the cross, "My God, My God, why have you forsaken me?" (Mark 15:34). This world has never heard such an agonized cry of loneliness. And this world will never again see such an example of submission to authority, largely because God raised Jesus from the grave. Because of the cross, we can live in reconciled community with God and with other believers.

Jesus-as-rebel just doesn't cut it. Jesus was in the first instance an obedient son and a loving friend.

When we listen to the message of the cross, we begin to really understand how Jesus-as-rebel just doesn't cut it. Jesus was in the first instance an obedient son and a loving friend. His rebellion was incidental to his greater purposes. A world gone to hell needs to see God's kingdom.

If we're going to find our way to healthy and full life, we cannot come to God with an attitude of control. Only God can resensitize our minds, soften our hearts and evaporate our cynicism. Every diversion and entertainment will eventually become boring. But by faith, God can transcend even boredom. He helps us laugh again. He replaces our shame with authenticity.

FAITH, HOPE AND LOVE

Throughout Jesus' public ministry, people swarmed around him. They liked the miracles, and they liked the free meals. But when Jesus got explicit about the true cost of following him, he lost many of his followers. It must have hurt him, because he then turned to ask his twelve disciples, "You do not want to leave too, do you?" Peter replies: "Lord, to whom else shall we go? You have the words of eternal life. We have come to believe and know that you are the Holy One of God" (John 6:67-69).

When we're honest with ourselves, we've got nothing. We are naked. We look like we've got everything. We put on our cool shades and project to the world that we've got it all together. *There's nothing to see here, folks; keep moving.* But Peter demonstrates to the other eleven disciples and to everyone through the centuries who has heard his reply, how to come to Jesus. "Lord, to whom else shall we go?"

We have nothing except Jesus. He has the way of eternal life. The sooner we accept this reality the healthier we will be. Eternal life is infinitely beyond anything we, as finite beings created to live in space and time, can touch on our own. And like everything else in God's kingdom, our interface with eternity is intangible and unexpected.

Magic can't last. Power can't last. Our bodies can't last. Cool certainly can't last. Paul writes: "Where there is knowledge, it will pass away. . . . For now we see only a reflection as in a mirror; then we shall see face to face. Now I know in part; then I shall know fully, even as I am fully known. And now these three remain: faith, hope and love. But the greatest of these is love" (1 Corinthians 13:8, 12-13). All we've got are faith, hope and love. The more we rely on these, the better off we'll be.

FAITH

Faith, the author of Hebrews tells us, "is being sure of what we hope for and certain of what we do not see" (Hebrews 11:1). Those of us with the privilege of the world's power and prestige can easily get blinded by our wealth. Faith is something intangible that connects us to eternity, a bridge spanning the chasm between the ruined lives we see around us and the reality of God's salvation and healing. Faith lets us look at suffering, confusion and hatred through the lens of the risen Christ. Faith is thus the beginning of God's reign.

Faith is both something we do and something God does for us. As a desperate father said, begging Jesus to heal his son, "I do believe, help me overcome my unbelief!" (Mark 9:24). Faith is something that can grow and mature, and like a friendship, it grows and matures from both sides.

Furthermore, faith is grounded in an understanding of God's character. It relates to memory of God's trustworthiness and love. After defining faith for us, the author of Hebrews continues through a lengthy history of faith, demonstrating throughout Hebrews 11 God's trustworthiness and the faith of those who've gone before us. Summarizing at the top of Hebrews 12, he says:

> Therefore, since we are surrounded by such a great cloud of witnesses, let us throw off everything that hinders and the sin that so easily entangles. And let us run with perseverance the race marked out for us, fixing our eyes on Jesus, the author and perfecter of faith. (Hebrews 12:1-2)

Faith is grounded in community (the great cloud surrounding us) and memory (the stories the witnesses have to tell). Faith single-mindedly focuses on Jesus. And faith helps us shed unnecessary baggage, like our fear of losing our cool.

Those who wonder what single-minded, naked faith looks like would do well to learn to live in Christian fellowship with the poor—

the great cloud of witnesses who "went about in sheepskins and goat-skins, destitute, persecuted and mistreated" (Hebrews 11:37). The poor have plenty of their own sin, but it is among the poor that we discover a stronger faith, hope and love than we had ever known.

There are many churches among the poor, of which Pentecostalism is only one. Pentecostalism is today the world's fastest-growing Christian body, with much of its growth coming in Latin America, Africa and Asia. It is also impossibly uncool. In North America, Pentecostal churches thrive among the poor, who too often feel ashamed to go to a "proper" church. The two largest Pentecostal organizations in the United States, the Church of God in Christ and the Assemblies of God, both trace their roots to one man—William Seymour—a black son of a slave who founded an intensely multiracial church in Los Angeles in 1906.

Pentecostal religion involves the human emotions in worship to a degree that often makes outsiders uncomfortable or skeptical. Indeed, Pentecostal faith is emotional enough that cool becomes nearly impossible—except from the back of the church. Many a person has lost his cool in such a church, dropping to his knees, crying out to God on behalf of his neighbors, calling down power from heaven or boldly claiming promises from Scripture. Although such displays have the potential of being shallow or showy, in their purest form they make cool seem cheap in comparison.

Many a person has lost his cool dropping to his knees, crying out to God.

Faith undermines fear. We see God's power, and we find ourselves surrounded by a great cloud of witnesses, so we no longer need to be afraid of the mess of the world. Faith gives us the power to drop our cool and get down in the dirt, into the suffering of the world, extending the beloved community to even the most disagreeable of souls.

HOPE

Then there is *hope*. Where faith connects us to God's trustworthiness throughout history, hope is supernatural power to connect to the coming glory, when Jesus will restore everything. Faith lets us touch the past; hope lets us touch the future.

Christian hope is not a situational hope, like a wish that the goalie will be able to handle the penalty kick or that the professor will grade on a curve. Rather, as Cornel West says, Christian hope is "grounded in the groundless mystery of the Cross—a prophetic . . . witness to the absurd love of Jesus Christ in a fallen world that views such love as folly and appears to reduce such love to impotence." Christian hope is a creative force, wrapped up in an understanding of God's character.

> **Hope gives us the power to drop our cool, because we no longer feel the need to measure ourselves by today's standards.**

This hope appears among even the most oppressed Christians throughout history. Christian hope is far more than resigning oneself to oppression. Theologian James Cone says:

> The idea of heaven was the means by which slaves affirmed their humanity in a world that did not recognize them as human beings. . . . Black slaves' hope in the coming justice of God was the chief reason they could hold themselves together in servitude and sometimes fight back, even though the odds were against them.

Because we have a future—because we have hope—shame's hold on us is broken in the here and now. Shame demands we live a lie, but hope liberates us, replacing our shame with authenticity. Hope gives us the power to drop our cool, because we no longer feel the need to measure ourselves by today's standards. We're no longer trapped in the moment.

LOVE

Finally, there is *love*. Faith anchors us in memory, hope connects us to the future, and between the two of them, love gives meaning and power to today. In the light of the church's collective memory of God's trustworthiness and the promise of eternal life, the here-and-now suddenly bursts with life. "There is no fear in love. But perfect love drives out fear" (1 John 4:18). Love crosses space and time. Love is the primary way in which we can see God's image among people: in our capacity to love and to be loved.

Built for eternity and characterized by love, the church is the central human actor in God's story of redemption. God is creating a people for himself, a community bound by love and sealed for eternity by the Holy Spirit. The church is God's masterpiece. He wants to show us off to the world.

When I first became a member of a church with a large underprivileged population, I didn't know what I was seeing. I thought I had just joined an African American church; so when I began to get exposed to the spiritual witness of the poor, I confused (as so many white folk do) culture and class. The miracle of reconciliation in my church is not that black, white, Asian and Latino Christians worship together, because we are far from out of the woods on that one. I would bet that no church in the world has it figured out entirely.

Cool will never be able to create a community like the church.

The real miracle of church is that the Holy Spirit has created a community out of sinful people, rich and poor alike, each of which was a train wreck before Jesus. Together, when Christians can open their hearts to each other in love, when the powerful can learn from the powerless, and those with means can serve those without, together we embody God's slow but sure march toward eternal wholeness and well-being.

Cool will never be able to create a community like the church:

weak and powerful, belonging yet apart, grounded in faith, hope and love.

RESTORATION AND RECONCILIATION

In the breaking of the bread, in the opening of our apartments and our hearts to each other, we remember Jesus' death and we celebrate communion—the eternal and real across space and time community. Reconciliation between people is a foretaste of heaven, and it is the surest evidence the world will ever see of the deeper reconciliation between God and sinners.

Our king commands his church to announce and collectively embody his reign. Our response must be to throw off anything that gets in the way and, as God's beloved community, venture into the heroin dens and crack houses of the world, into the sick and broken dormitories of the world, into the savage and hostile workplaces of the world, to announce the presence of the king.

> Heal the sick who are there and tell them, "the kingdom of God
> has come near to you." (Luke 10:9)

While I was in college, I worked a number of manual labor jobs, from roofing to snow removal to landscaping. It was good for me. I learned a work ethic; I learned all kinds of everyday skills, like how to load a dump truck and how to blast swarms of angry hornets out of the air with cans of Raid—without falling off the roof. I also learned valuable social skills, like when it's appropriate to join a conversation in progress with a quote from Immanuel Kant (never) and how to sign your coworkers out of the county jail.

Alongside this education, a more subtle change was going on: my hands got callused. After I had first spent a few days of hauling wheelbarrows full of concrete, my soft college-boy hands were a throbbing, blistered wreck. But I ignored the blisters. I needed the work, and I was too proud to quit anyway. My coworkers had dedicated my first week to telling me that college boys didn't know how to work real jobs. I was so determined to prove them wrong that I never noticed my hands developing a healthy layer of protection—hard and insensitive skin. Callus is a good thing; it makes manual labor possible.

Doubtless Jesus had hard-as-steel hands. After a quarter-century of carpentry, three years of ministry wouldn't undo all that good clean hard work. Callus isn't like a summer tan, which goes away after a few weeks. Although toughened skin scrapes away after weeks of inaction (much like book-learning), callused skin is changed skin. Your skin seems to carry a memory of callus, and for the rest of your life, if you no more than spend an afternoon with a shovel, your calluses will come back overnight. It's a miracle, really.

Callus is an important part of the natural order. When we get scraped, we toughen up. When we get cut, we scar up. When we get attacked on the inside, we build up an immune resistance. It's a miracle. But in a fallen world, drowning in its own mess, the same hardness also attacks our hearts. When we get abused, we turn hard. When we open our hearts, only to be crushed, we get a lot more protective of our hearts. The evil out there in the world calluses our hearts, because our hearts are too tender to bear it all.

Cool is a form of callus. But the way of Jesus is not to get tougher or stouter of heart but to grow in love and hope and faith. True compassion lives at the level of suffering. At the level of suffering, among the broken-hearted crying alone in concrete stairwells, among the doped-up broken lives, among the violent trapped in cycles of violence and among the sexually abusive, trapped in cycles of sexual abuse—at that level of suffering, God sends his church. Because of our hope, we no longer have to protect our other cheek. Liberated from the need to protect ourselves, he sends us out into the world with bigger hearts. And can we ever feel the pain!

6

REENCHANTMENT

Losing Our Cool in the Church, the Family and the Heart

"Do you have any Africa in you?" Sister Fabu asked me. We were at Wisconsin's State Historical Museum, looking at an exhibit on immigration. Hanging on the wall before us was an 1870 census map of Wisconsin. It depicted, by Wisconsin township, the Old World countries of origin of the foreign-born population, which in that year constituted 68 percent of the state's residents. Germans, Poles, Irish, Swedes, Swiss, Belgians and others each had their own shading on the map.

"Not that I'm aware of," I replied, fairly certain the answer was no. My father's family has been in the New World since the early 1600s. That side of my family was English, Scottish and Irish; my mother's side was made up of twentieth-century Scandinavian immigrants. I'm a mutt, to be sure, but there was no Africa in my blood.

Fabu Mogaka, an African-American poet, educator and overall wise woman, had hired me to tutor children that summer, but for the moment she was more focused on me than on the children, who were plenty occupied with more interesting, hands-on exhibits.

"Then you're looking at it all wrong," she said with a twinkle in her eye. "You're looking at blood. You like country music, don't you?"

I knew where she was going with this and started to feel my white cheeks flush red.

"You like rock music, don't you?"

I nodded. Then, with a smile that doubled as congratulation and compassion, she delivered the punch line.

"Then you've got lots of Africa in you. Your heart is beating to the rhythms of the ancient African drums."

I was humiliated and astonished. She had caught me focusing on DNA instead of the heart.

Love, not blood, is at the center of the soul. The body is important too: not even the strictest mind-body dualists would claim that my light-skinned, healthy and fully functional six-foot male frame has no impact on my self-perception. But as Christians—who believe that we have been adopted into God's family (Ephesians 1:5); who believe we are the answer to God's promise to Abraham—we believe that belonging is not merely genetic but spiritual (Romans 4:16). The church is God's family, adopted by grace out of our families of origin, and into Abraham's family. It is a miracle.

Our adoption is the foundation of Christian love and crosscultural fellowship. Our adoption is the basis of our hope, our new identity as the church: the *ekklesia* in Greek, we are the *called out*. God has set us apart from the world, even from our blood families. He gives us a new name—his name. The church is the basis of our belonging, the basis for our blessed uncool. Uncool alone can't change the world, but the church can and does.

Uncool alone can't change the world, but the church can and does.

Reenchantment is about the return of the sacred to a disenchanted world. In the broader cultural landscape, reenchantment usually means finding something spiritual and imputing it into the profane areas of our lives. It can also mean refurbishing with spiritual power areas of our lives—including religion, our minds and our bodies—where it is missing.

Reenchantment in this worldly sense is both an acknowledgment of our spiritual incompleteness and an assertion of our individual authority over our own spiritual lives. But we can no more conquer our souls from within than we can conquer other peoples' souls from without. Christians assert something different: any reenchantment that comes our way is a gift from God. God has been here all along, quite actively building a beloved community for himself. God reenchants the church; the church does not reenchant God.

DISENCHANTMENT

No matter how we define reenchantment, we are implicitly referring to an earlier event: disenchantment. There are of course many types of disenchantment, and not all are compatible with cool. As concerns cool, there is a disenchantment native to the industrialized world of rational, bureaucratic government and commerce—to the world we live in.

At the beginning of the twentieth century, German sociologist Max Weber produced what remains the seminal work on disenchantment: *The Protestant Ethic and the Spirit of Capitalism*. He wanted to know if any room for human dignity remained in an industrial, bureaucratic world, a world trapped in an "iron cage" of "mechanized petrification, embellished with a sort of convulsive self-importance. For of the last stage of [capitalism's] development, it might well be truly said: Specialists without spirit, sensualists without heart."

For Weber disenchantment was the flight of the spiritual world from our culture, a flight that turned us into something less than fully human. Disenchantment is the consequence of human attempts to bring order and control to the spontaneous and random aspects of life through the media of bureaucracy and rationality.

To a certain extent, cool as we now know it presupposes a disenchanted world. Remember that cool's West African origins emphasize the individual's mastery over circumstances, both in attitude and in action. Throughout its long career in the New World, hipsters have continually tried to comprehend and trick the authorities, in order to bring some semblance of order and control to a chaotic world, and to bring a sensation of individual significance to a landscape of "mechanized petrification."

Cool as we now know it presupposes a disenchanted world.

Cool is a lifeline for many disenchanted people, so we shouldn't be surprised at cool's continual reappearance, even in our own Christian lives. Old habits die hard, especially when those habits have taproots that reach the soul. The good news is that enchantment can return to the world. Sometimes it appears spontaneously, like those moments when four-lane highways slow to a halt to allow a mother duck to lead her downy-yellow brood across to safety. Other times we choose reenchantment, like when we fall in love. Unfortunately, the world is much bigger than baby ducks and puppy love. In the face of the most grotesque human depravities, anything less than miraculous won't suffice.

SELF-CENTERED REENCHANTMENT

Americans in particular, at once an intensely individualistic and spiritually insatiable people, have sponsored several attempts at reenchantment in a few short centuries. Asian spirituality, from yoga to Feng Shui, has made continual breakthroughs into the American mainstream. Drug fads have come and gone, each promising some version of enlightenment through individual experience. Native American religions are currently booming, but as Philip Jenkins notes in *Dream Catchers*, non-native participants in native religions deethnicize ethnic rituals, creating a new religion that is much more individualistic in nature. Practitioners can play as deeply as they desire in this mystical, new-age religion, with minimal communal demands, and return to the office on Monday, without messy relational problems to worry about.

And that is the common ingredient: From astrology to Zen, disenchanted folk will do anything for a taste of the really real, as long as they can do it alone. Even communal faiths, such as Wicca, proudly advertise their non-hierarchical qualities. *For God's sake*, the American soul says, *don't make me submit to anything or anyone.*

These millions of American seekers didn't drop out of the sky. Most of them have come out of the Christian church. Many were only Christian in name, having inherited their faith from their families, but a sizeable body of former believers in Jesus count themselves among the spiritually seeking. Others, however, are sticking it out and trying to reenchant the faith while remaining true to Jesus. They often pay great attention to the legacy of faith the church has inherited from old traditions; Celtic Christianity, first-century Judaism and medieval monasticism have all received loving tributes from these Christians. They have discovered that the solution to a predictable, boring faith is relinquishing control over God and salvation.

A choice presents itself to disenchanted folk. Reenchantment begins the moment we confess: our salvation was never in our own hands in the first place. Will we allow God to pry open our lonely and alienated souls? Do we trust him enough?

LOVE UNTIL DEATH

God is the same yesterday, today and forever, so only a faith that is reconciled with yesterday and tomorrow can know God. And since cool lives only in the present, it is only by rejecting cool that we can truly become reconciled with the past and with the future. We cannot grow into Christian maturity by denying the progression of time.

Perhaps the best American novel of the last quarter-century is Don DeLillo's *White Noise*. The book follows a year in the life of a professor at a small liberal arts college as he tries to make sense of his students, his family and the consumer world around him. Over and over, the question comes up: why do we feel such a need to fill our lives with white noise? Why must we always surround ourselves with sensual stimuli such as television, food, advertising and more? Through a brilliant and ridiculous course of events, DeLillo's Jack Gladney stumbles across the answer: we entertain ourselves to death because we can't deal with death. We've mastered outer space and have nearly eliminated hunger, but death remains intimately close to the human experience.

Cardinal Robert Bellarmine, the seventeenth century Jesuit most known as Galileo's prosecutor, was also a profound thinker on the meaning of life. He writes in his book *The Art of Dying Well,* "One should live well if one desires to die well, . . . for since death is merely the end of life, surely everyone who lives well up to the end cannot die badly, since he has never lived badly, just as he who has always lived badly dies badly." In other words, the good life takes the end of life into account throughout.

We no longer have many cultural resources to face death— certainly none as boldly prescriptive as Robert Bellarmine's—so we resort to entertainment and white noise. To rephrase Bellarmine, if we can't face death, we can't face life, and we certainly can't risk loving other people, because love lingers at the deathbed.

HELL IS A COOL PLACE

While love is lingering on the deathbed, however, cool is glorying in death and the underworld. Popular images of heaven range from esoteric realms of undifferentiated light, to trite and colorless cloud scenes, bereft of furniture, trees or just about any human artifacts save harps. Heaven is decidedly boring and unappealing. Hell, in popular imagination, looks a lot like earth. Hell has funk bands and flashy clothes. Hell is cool, in the coolest sense of the word.

When did hell become more interesting than heaven? Beyond the level of caricatures lies a serious faith problem: if heaven is sterile, if our hope lies in an unsalty eternity serving a dour God who hates colors, diversity, wild passions or laughter, then living for today and celebrating an eternity separated from such a God is a rational course of action. Fortunately, Christian hope is not empty. God is building a blessed community for himself with as varied a population as exists on earth. And when God sets everything right at the end, it will be the memory of life on earth that seems boring in contrast to the tangible, creative, vibrant community surrounding the risen Christ. In place of the oppressive and segregated planet Earth, "on no day will [the New Jerusalem's] gates be shut, for there will be no night there. The glory and honor of the nations will be brought into it" (Revelation 21:25-26). Since the glory and honor of the nations would presumably include food, music, modes of humor and other cultural artifacts, our eternal hope is for an authentic and intensely colorful home, endlessly astonishing and enchanting. Today's earth is the real drag.

REENCHANTED LOVE

A reenchanted hope makes for a reenchanted now. God created us for love. Community, not cosmic aloneness, is his nature. And the salvation he brings to a lost and dying world manifests itself in reconciliation—which is right relationships and community.

John put it eloquently: "Love comes from God. Everyone who loves has been born of God and knows God. Whoever does not love does not know God" (1 John 4:7-8). In other words, it is not when we are most morally pure, or most prophetic, that we are at our godliest: it is when we love as God loves.

How does God love? He sent his Son to die for us. God's love is not pain free. Disenchantment is a natural reaction to a lack of real love. Reenchantment happens when God's love—all-risking, soft-hearted, open-armed love—comes to his church and from there goes out to the disenchanted world. Reenchantment is therefore a blessing with strings attached: inasmuch as we are loved, God also expects us to love.

Not surprisingly, considering its relationship to love, reenchantment is also a cooperative venture: something we do together with
God. Reenchantment includes a willful element on our part, an insis-
tence on seeing God's fingerprint in God's world. But it is much more
about God opening our eyes to see what is already there. The farther
we travel in faith, the more faith God gives us. And the more faith God
gives us, the more Christlike and mature we become.

OUR FAMILY TREE

Mature literally means ripe, so *spiritually mature* means full of ripe
spiritual fruit. White-haired, wrinkled inner beauty begins with spiritual discipline in the flower of youth. Retired missionaries, people
who've upheld their families in prayer for generations and other mature followers of Christ have a magical quality about them. They seem
simultaneously otherworldly and down-to-earth.

Once we stop worrying about looking good, the Bible sounds different to our reenchanted ears, and we see new windows of opportunity for bringing reconciliation to broken relationships. Revelation
and reconciliation: these are close to God's heart. Throughout Scripture, God reveals himself as intrinsically committed to relationships.
He lives in a three-in-one community with himself, and he lives in
covenantal relationships with his people.

One of the most astonishing stories in the Bible is that of God's covenant with Abraham, as recorded in Genesis 15. In ancient Middle
Eastern culture,

> the contracting parties to a covenant performed a solemn rite to
> symbolize the sacredness of their pledge. Sacrificial animals
> were halved and placed in such a way as to enable the covenant-
> ing persons to pass between the carcasses. By doing so they
> acted out an oath and declared themselves liable to the fate of
> the animals should they break the terms of the agreement.

God instructs Abraham to prepare the scene for the ritual. The slaughtered cattle is bisected and laid out on the ground. So far so good. But then God does something incredible. As Abraham lies in a deep sleep, he watches as God, in the form of a torch and a smoking pot, passes *alone* between the carcasses. In other words, God has unilaterally entered into the covenant. Abraham does nothing but chase away some birds trying to eat the dead animals; the Creator of the universe, the only autonomous agent in existence, binds his eternal fate to that of Abraham and Abraham's descendents!

Thus begins a pattern continuing to this day: God seems to think that right relationships are non-negotiable. God works through people to accomplish his purposes for the world. And unfortunately for those of us who prefer to be self-determined, God ministers to us through other people. Conversely, his purposes for other people include roles for us. Our commitment to God is inseparable from our commitment to God's people. Life's journey is thus part of salvation. God works through people because that is the nature of his kingdom.

Our lives, our relationships, and our families do not stand on their own. We belong to others. As Christians, we belong to Christ. We are God's gift to Abraham—the fulfillment of the promise he made thousands of years ago: "Look up at the heavens and count the stars—if indeed you can count them. . . . So shall your offspring be" (Genesis 15:5). God has never stopped chasing us—throughout our lives and throughout history. Our story is part of Abraham's story, and Abraham's story is part of God's story. We know this because the Bible, God's record of self-revelation, tells us so.

God's story is thus not just about relationships in the moment; it is also about relationships through time. When we are cool, we nearly lose the ability to relate to others through time. In May 2005, millions of Americans lined up to see the final installation of the *Star Wars* series of movies. Presumably the majority of the first weekend's viewers were not standing in line in order to have their lingering questions answered, because everyone knew the outcome in advance: Anakin Skywalker was going to become Darth Vader. The question was not one of mystery, but one of *story*. People wanted to hear the story they'd grown up with, told with new details. They wanted to spend two hours with old friends.

In the same way, the great drama of Scripture is not that of the unknown but the known. It is the ever-fresh story of God's project to create for himself a people with whom he would live forever. The magic is in the telling and the retelling. Is the Bible boring? Try taking a deep immersion in the Bible's story itself. As we begin to embrace history, and as we grow in our understanding of love, the Bible reveals its wonderful secret: God's story is our family's story too. The Bible is our family tree.

OUR FAMILY TODAY

Twenty-first century Christians stand on the shoulders of far more saints than those mentioned in the Bible. To acquaint oneself with church history is to meet one's parents. Those who've gone before us make it easier for us to live our faith, because we see in their legacy the church's progress along the race laid before it. And if nearly three thousand years ago King Solomon was able to say, "There is nothing new under the sun," how much more true is that today? It is a particular American conceit, wrapped up with our existential individualism, that we are unlike anyone before us, and that today's problems are unlike those faced by people before us. King Solomon did not live to see cloning, egg donations, plastic surgery, brain-dead hospital patients, nuclear waste or other technology-wrought moral questions, but human nature remains substantially the same as in his day, and the real questions of life and death are the same. At most we have to tweak or interpret what our ancestors already discovered. There is no human development we can possibly think of that hasn't already been addressed by other Christians. The same holds true across space: the church today is far healthier than we realize. But since our relational muscles are underdeveloped, we rarely tap into the church's accumulated experience, preferring instead to deal with new issues on our own.

We all need history. More precisely, we need memory. Without memory, our souls die faster than our bodies. Without a firm sense of history— not so much the *facts* of history but the logic of time itself—without a vision of a historical Savior's movement in relation to his creation, we are less than fully human. Memory connects us to the living church; when we go it alone we risk losing everything: even our identities.

The danger in the American church is less that we believe the wrong beliefs than that we believe them all by ourselves.

The danger in the American church is less that we believe the wrong beliefs than that we believe them all by ourselves, in the absence of community in space or time. We learn much more about God through the eyes of other believers than on our own. Living in history is much more enchanting than inventing new religions or spiritualities. On the one hand, there is nothing wrong in reshaping our churches to become more relevant to the needs of each generation, but this innovation has to be done in love. Before, for instance, we reinvent ourselves according to the spiritual disciplines of ancient Celtic saints, we might sit down with our own parents, asking them about their own spiritual experience.

MEET THE PARENTS

My mother never let me be cool. As a fifteen-year old, I really wanted to walk ten feet behind her at the department store, lest I be seen with her. Little did I know that I was only going through a stage. Then she told me. Some mothers get annoyed at their teenagers' disassociation and force them to heel. My mother did something worse: she explained my immaturity to me. It's hard to look cool and mature when you know that your devices themselves are immature. My mother saved me from myself. By appealing not to her parental authority but to our common human experience, she bridged a generation gap before it really developed. And by giving me an understanding of common suffering—teenagers' emerging adulthood and the parental separation that entails—she enabled me to avoid the worst of teenage rebellion.

More challenging than standard teenage rebellion, yet containing more potential for enriching the church, is intergenerational dialogue between immigrant teenagers and their parents. All parents suffer through their children's rebellion, but because of the culture gap between the first and second generations of immigrants, mutual comprehension between parents and rebellious teenagers is much more difficult (and supernatural when it happens). While cultural treasures are always lost in translation, immigrant children have the opportunity to bridge both worlds, and bring to both an understanding of God's mercy and the church's riches.

God's fingerprints can be uniquely seen in each culture's experience. When people from different cultures share the gospel with one another, both get to know God in new ways. Cool has never done well with culture, because culture implies belonging. But when we reject cool's starting points, favoring instead faith, hope and love, culture gains new life. Since belonging to others compromises our cool, that's exactly where we should go: we can learn from, and can receive from, people we otherwise would have avoided or ignored in the beloved community. Crosscultural fellowship, nearly impossible under cool, becomes one of God's tools for reenchanting the church: as we live in reconciled love with believers from other countries, generations and denominations, we walk with wide-open eyes, astonished at the beautiful bride God is creating.

Uncool humility allows us to listen to the stories and enjoy the witness the Chinese church has developed under persecution. Faith in

God's provision for everyone frees us to submit to the agenda of the poor church in North America. Love demands we approach our alienated fellow believers with soft hearts and open hands. And as Sister Fabu understood years before me, love makes it possible for me to celebrate those to whom I belong.

7

COMPASSION

When to Care What the World Thinks

"Whore! Slut!" What a way to start a sermon.

There she stood on a sidewalk on campus between classes, in her ankle-length flower-print dress, Bible in one hand. This left her other hand free to point at passersby and call out random sins. "Idolater! . . . Homosexual!"

I'd seen her before. She and her husband showed up on campus every spring, coinciding with the reappearance of migratory water-fowl and summer dresses. Rumor had it they made a preaching tour of all the Big Ten campuses. If you're out to address the moral vacuity of today's youth, I suppose those schools could be a good place to start.

Having quickly amassed a wealth of hostility in the form of a circle of jeering spectators, with herself at the center and a radius of about fifteen feet, she commenced her sermon proper. I have no idea what she said. I doubt anyone else remembers either. Her person spoke louder than her words.

After five years of hearing their sermons twice a year (they also passed through in the fall), I was able to cobble together a bit of her theology. She never explained what made someone a whore, or why being a whore was bad, or how to stop being a whore. All these complexities would presumably resolve themselves upon repentance from whoring. Their key concern was biblical purity. And therein lay their methodological error: at a school like Wisconsin, with thousands of international students, Jews and atheists, they shouldn't have counted on people having had a childhood foundation in Sunday school. They overestimated both the respect and the knowledge students had of Jesus. Had this lady been preaching on the campus of a Christian college, or in the pulpit of a church, she would be following Jesus' model much more closely: Jesus reserved his harshest words for those with the most solid background in Scripture; those who should know better. (In Matthew 12:34 he addresses them with "You brood of vipers, how can you who are evil say anything good?")

At some point that afternoon, the crowd must have gotten unruly, because the preacher lady interrupted herself to accuse more people of assorted sins. I was never sure if she merely picked sins out of a hat, or if she tried to read specific guilt off individuals' faces. Not that it matters a great deal, because if anyone felt convicted, they certainly didn't show it.

Curious to see which sin I'd committed, I timed my path past the preacher lady to get her maximum attention. She was in a rhythm: One-two-three-four. "Drunkard! . . . Liar! . . . Thief!" I timed it right; she spotted me. As I strode past, pretending not to see her, her arthritic hand rose in my direction, finger ready. "Forrrrnicatorrr!" she trilled.

Now I should make it clear that I was no fornicator. It was a false accusation. So I should have been upset, but I wasn't. Rather I felt like I'd just slain the stage boss in an old Nintendo game: figure out the pattern and go for the kill. If it were merely a game, then I had won. But it wasn't a game. For many students, this was their first and possibly last exposure to Christianity.

The preacher lady and her husband invariably drew verbal abuse from the crowd, but they seemed to savor it. Perhaps they were rejoicing in their persecution. Perhaps they thought that the substance of the Great Commission was contained in words alone. I don't know what they were thinking. But this I know: sometimes, the world doesn't hate us for Christ's sake. Sometimes the world hates Christians because we're being big jerks.

Sometimes the world hates Christians because we're being big jerks.
When the church quietly goes about its business of faith, hope and love, revolutionary forces get unleashed, and those opposed to the revolution will react and resist. Obedience to the gospel leads to the world's hatred. But sometimes we Christians confuse cause and effect. The world's hatred is aroused by many things other than obedience to the gospel. Just because the world today hates Adolf Hitler doesn't mean he was a great disciple of Jesus.

Jesus promised his disciples they'd be persecuted for their faith. But this persecution would come as a consequence of the threat Christian faith poses to the established order. To lift up the poor is high treason to a social order interested in keeping them poor. To restore dignity to the degraded is threatening to a degrading status quo. And to pronounce purity upon violated women is offensive to those who violated them in the first place.

Calling random women whores and sluts is not helpful to the gospel. An outrageous number of college students get raped each year, and far too many are forced to rebuild their lives on their own. They need the compassionate Jesus, the one who called the woman with a menstrual disorder "daughter" (Luke 8:48). It's hard for us today to understand the power of taboos on the social standing of outsiders like this ritually unclean woman; in many cases, even family wouldn't speak to unclean people. But Jesus called her "daughter."

Survivors of rape, who have to rebuild their lives on their own in a compassionless world, women who are often haunted by doubts about their own participation in the crime, need the Jesus who defended the woman caught in adultery—the Jesus who dared "any one of [her accusers] who is without sin to be the first to throw a stone at her" (John 8:7).

In a world in which beastly masculinity is considered cool, in a world whose airwaves are crammed with chart-topping songs calling women bitches and whores, young women need *Immanuel*, God-with-us.

Christ loved us while we were yet sinners. After saving the woman caught in adultery from certain death, he told her to "go now and leave your life of sin" (John 8:11). Clearly Jesus was not weak on hard truth. But Jesus was primarily concerned with announcing God's kingdom, and his gentleness and his harshness alike flowed out of an overarching compassion for lost humanity. If we're going to follow Christ's example, we're going to have to treat the world with the same kind of compassion that he did.

THE INEFFICIENCY OF LOVE

Compassion has always been one of the gospel's best modes of trans-mission. But it rarely makes for good strategy. In a market-driven world, efficiency is the primary virtue. The best strategies are the most efficient means to profit. The market derives its rationality from scar-city: resources are scarce, so we have to do the best with what we have.

Even the church values efficiency. Healthy, well-adjusted people are more efficient to reach than needy, wounded and seriously messed up people. Even though the well-off may live with significant pain, the downtrodden—who frequently lack any safety nets—often re-quire much more ongoing ministry and service. If so-and-so many people are lost but easy to reach over here, and the same number of people are lost but much harder to reach over there, the principle of efficiency is clear: go for the former. We minister to college students because they are tomorrow's leaders; to international students be-cause if they accept the gospel they will return to their home country (preferably a staunchly non-Christian one) as a homegrown missionary; to cool people because they will attract uncool people by virtue of their cool charisma. It's a value judgment that resonates with our culture: The cool-driven market treats people as commodities; compassion treats them as people.

We minister to cool people because they will attract uncool people by virtue of their cool charisma. It's a value judgment that resonates with our culture.

Cool and efficiency both view the world through the lens of scarcity, but the bounty of God's economy makes many of our strategies irrelevant. In God's economy, there are unlimited resources and therefore efficiency is not a value. Money does not grow on trees—but love might. Love defies the laws of thermodynamics: love can generate more love *ex nihilo*, out of thin air. Love can be lavished, and if nothing else, compassion is lavish.

Like Jesus, who spent most of his time with commoners, we go where God's love impels us— which is not necessarily strategic or efficient. Compassion drops everything to serve those in need. Not all students are tomorrow's leaders, but all students need love. We should reach cool people for Christ not because they're strategic but because they're often lonely and suffering. If we don't care how good we look, we can go wherever God calls us, even if it's somewhere where ministry is tedious and painstaking. Strategic thinking can easily turn beautiful and intelligent people into mere numbers. Love turns those numbers into friends.

COMPASSION: SUFFERING ALONG-WITH

Compassion derives from the Latin words *cum* (with), and *pati* (suffering). Compassion literally means "suffering along-with." Compassion is suffering with a twist: it is fellowship in suffering.

And suffering is reality. Ever since Adam and Eve introduced rebellion into human life, human life has been a constant stream of anguish and sorrow. Suffering goes deep into the soul, deeper than cool's capacity to mask it, deeper than drugs' capacity to numb it, or entertainment's capacity to drown it out.

But as deep as the human condition goes, God can reach down there, and other people can too—through our capacity to love. As surely as God took on the skin and bones of a common carpenter and lived a life with us, so he can also understand and speak into the most basic human realities.

Amazingly, God doesn't always lift us out, or take away the pain, or make that someone love us—but he is always with us. He is not afraid of our pain. Compassion is fellowship—or love—where there is suffering. When we say God is a compassionate God, we mean that he is with us.

Compassion has its origin in God, and its most clear model in the person of Jesus. A beautiful description of God's compassion for us in Jesus is found in one of the first church songs recorded—in Paul's letter to the church in Philippi, which he wrote from a Roman prison. "In your relationships with one another," Paul says,

Have the same attitude of mind Christ Jesus had:
  Who, being in very nature God,
    Did not consider equality with God something to be used
to his own advantage;
  rather, he made himself nothing
    by taking the very nature of a servant,
    being made in human likeness.
And being found in appearance as a human being,
    he humbled himself
    by becoming obedient to death—even death on a cross!
Therefore God exalted him to the highest place
    and gave him the name that is above every name,
that at the name of Jesus every knee should bow,

in heaven and on earth and under the earth,
and every tongue acknowledge that Jesus Christ is lord,
to the glory of God the Father. (Philippians 2:6-11)

Jesus isn't merely compassionate; his compassionate service and humility proves to us his divinity. God demonstrates his love for us by suffering.

When I entered college as a freshman, I felt that philosophical defense of the gospel was the only way to reach the campus. Accordingly, I stacked my curriculum with philosophy classes, to better argue people into the kingdom. But God melted my cool arrogance. Three Catholic priests—Henri Nouwen, Donald McNeill and Douglas Morrison—wrote a response to the deadness of academic life compared with the magnitude of the world's suffering. Their wonderful little book *Compassion: a Reflection on the Christian Life* literally changed my life.

At first glance, compassion looks a lot like pity or sympathy, but there is a world of difference between the two. Pity tries to snuff out suffering; compassion transcends it altogether. Pity reaches down from on high to still the sufferers' agony. Pity doesn't care who the victims are, just as long as they'll stop crying. "On the contrary," Nouwen, McNeill and Morrison write,

> compassion means going directly to those people and those places where suffering is most acute and building a home there. God's compassion is total, absolute, unconditional, without reservation. It is the compassion of the one who keeps going to the forgotten corners of the world, and who cannot rest as long as he knows that there are still human beings with tears in their eyes. It is the compassion of a God who does not merely act as a servant, but whose servanthood is a direct expression of his divinity.

I began to understand that truth needs to be complemented with compassion. The Christian life is lived down in the dirt.

COURAGEOUS COMPASSION

Compassion is thus not for the timid. Living by God's power makes us infinitely courageous, and not just in terms of risk to life and limb. The prophet Jonah, the most famous grump in the Bible, initially refused his mission from God by fleeing for his life. God had told him to venture to Assyria's capital city Nineveh and "preach against it, because its wickedness has come up before me" (Jonah 1:2). Assyria was at the time the world's only superpower, with a reputation for brutality. In terms of the terror they inflicted on their enemies, Assyrians made the terrorists we have today seem second-rate.

With over 120,000 people, Assyria's capital city Nineveh was enormous by ancient Middle Eastern standards. Going into such a city in such an empire with a message of repentance would have been incredibly courageous, if not foolhardy. The Assyrians didn't just kill people. They made sure to hurt you first.

But Jonah didn't want the Ninevites to hear from God, because he didn't want them to repent and thus be spared the calamity he felt was due them. Jonah tried to manipulate God into raining down punishment on Nineveh. But that wasn't a real workable strategy, God being the judge, after all. Jonah's worst fear became reality: Nineveh repented, and God relented. And Jonah was mad about it.

> Isn't this what I said, Lord, when I was still at home? This is what I tried to forestall by fleeing to Tarshish. I knew that you are a gracious and compassionate God, slow to anger and abounding in love, a God who relents from sending calamity. Now, Lord, take away my life, for it is better for me to die than to live. (Jonah 4:2-3)

From our perspective, God's compassion seems to be unreasonably strong. Jonah's anger has a familiar ring to it. His experience forces us to ask: Are there any people alive we would deny a chance to repent? Is there anyone so despicable that we can't muster the compassion to invite them to repentance? Are there any perpetrators out there whose crimes are so great that we want to see nothing but hellfire heaped upon them?

Here is our problem: we want justice for the oppressed without justice for perpetrators. We are all sinners and equal recipients of grace. This *solidarity in sin,* theologian Miroslav Volf points out, is distinct from *equality of sin*—which would let perpetrators off the hook. As long as we are focused on our own relative innocence, we shudder to acknowledge our common human evil. It doesn't seem fair that perpetrators of evil could receive salvation when they repent—until we recognize our solidarity in sin through the lens of compassion.

Who are the perpetrators of the greatest evil in the world? Bangkok might be a decent place to start looking. Thailand's prostitution industry is as despicable as it is enormous. Bangkok is the epicenter of a global market in sexual tourism. Across North America, Europe and Asia, semi-underground travel agencies provide all-inclusive sex tourist trips to Bangkok. I had a friend in high school whose parents sent him there for his sixteenth birthday; their vision of manhood was tied up with prostitution. Thai girls are the objects of an entire world's ravenous lust. And girls they are—many are prepubescent when they begin their sentences. A significant number of these girls are virtual slaves, having been sold by parents in financial dire straits. They spend their days hidden from the world and forgotten, and their nights exposed to the world's ugliest side.

As I was thinking about compassion, I went to a large missions convention and sought out missions agencies doing work in Thailand. As I walked around among the missionaries, I found many opportunities for ministry among the girls of Bangkok—but none for ministry among the perpetrators. Was anyone doing ministry in

Bangkok's infamous brothels—among the clientele?

The answer was a resounding no. But the reason turned out to be more complicated than mere lack of compassion—and gave me a new perspective on how profound human sin is, and how holistic God's healing is. One missionary said, "We don't do ministry with the Johns because our missionaries burn out." After a certain time spent salving the trauma of girls-turned-objects for the world's rich and powerful, missionaries are understandably reluctant to divert limited resources to the men inflicting that trauma on the girls.

I found my hot anger about the commercialization in Bangkok of what God designed for marriage turning into compassion. Who are these men? Each of them is some mother's son. Each of them is known—down to the depths of his soul—by his Creator. As much as sex tourists are perpetrators of misery, they are also victims in their own right, trapped in compulsions and perversions. Even as they have sex with slaves and children, they too are captives. Even more than they need to be stopped in their toxic hobby, Bangkok's perpetrators need a Savior.

If the church is the only Jesus this hurting world will be able to see, the church will need to go into every hell-hole with his compassion. In provoking my passion for these sinners, was God calling me? I'm still trying to figure this one out. So far I've concluded that the solution starts here. Ground zero for all of the abuse happening in Thailand is wherever the abusers themselves are created. That place is nearly everywhere today—in our homes and offices, in front of a computer or a TV screen. Men don't morph into callus abusers in dark allies and seedy joints. Their degradation comes softly and tenderly over a period of years, as their sexuality gets destroyed. Healthy people don't fall in Bangkok's brothels; their fall comes way earlier.

One year I was living in the dorms, several young men—boys, really—thought it'd be clever and cool to take over the floor lounge on Wednesday nights to show pornographic movies on the big screen TV. These students gathered for what they came to call "Porn Night" to feast their eyes on broken minds and broken bodies, to glory in the objectification and dehumanization of women their same age. At the same time, their souls were growing more callused to femininity and beauty.

Pornography is cool: it projects effortless mastery of others without consequences. And since cool is such an unquestionable good in our culture, objecting to pornography is bewildering to many people today. It is as if one is questioning gender itself. But compassion, which gives voices to the voiceless, cannot make concessions to pornography.

Jesus once said, "Everyone who sins is a slave to sin. Now a slave has no permanent place in the family, but a son belongs to it forever. So if the Son sets you free, you are free indeed" (John 8:34-36). Here in Witte Hall, young men and women who thought themselves cool, enlightened and sexually liberated were gaining their liberation at the expense of the women on TV. But they were also growing increasingly acclimated to warped visions of intimacy. Pornography, according to Pamela Paul, makes men far less compassionate toward women and less likely to support women's causes in general.

Ground zero for Bangkok's brothels is wherever men are being trained (or are training themselves) to objectify women and girls, or wherever some mother's son is being inoculated against a woman's feelings. Ground zero is Witte Hall. I am not saying that Porn Night in Witte Hall forces Thai farmers to sell their daughters to bar-owners. But human sexuality has far more power over our souls (male and female alike) than we can ever fully comprehend. Left unguarded, our sexuality has a habit of leading us to do things we could never imagine. That's why so many war crimes involve sexual torture: let the cruelty beast out of the cage, and it'll pull on all our creative faculties. If not causally, Porn Night on campus and Thailand's red light districts are nevertheless closely related. All those all-inclusive travel agencies have got millions of dollars riding on the connection.

The evangelical church has always been big on sexual morality (not very cool) and is increasingly concerned about justice (sometimes cool, sometimes not). Being judgmental, on the other hand, is very uncool in the eyes of contemporary society. But when people are living in hell, the compassionate God-with-us has much bigger priorities than worrying about looking cool and not looking judgmental. So, should the beloved community care about sex slavery in Southeast Asia? Then should the beloved community start making some noise about Porn Night?

SUFFERING STRANGERS

The real world is chock full of suffering and grief. Jesus knew how to linger in grief, and to feel the feelings of loss. But by giving us the illusion of impenetrability, cool deprives us of the privilege of listening to, grieving with and restoring to health those whose eyes have seen all kinds of hell.

For every soldier who returns from conflict and successfully reenters civilian life, surrounded by family, there are others who have no one to welcome them. A new genre of music is bubbling up from American barracks in Iraq: Soldier Rap. Soldiers are making new music because they no longer feel that American pop culture speaks to them. They tell their stories to each other (and post them on the web for whoever cares to listen). In their August 2004 song recorded in Iraq, "Stay in Step," an outfit called Corner Pocket said:

> It's not easy being a soldier
> Never knowing if today's the day
> You're going to Hell or Heaven.

So far, this is hardly different than any other tough-guy talk. Rapper 50 Cent has made a career off his backstory of gang violence. "Fiddy" has famously been shot multiple times, and has made millions of dollars for each bullet wound. For 50 Cent and others like him, violence, thuggery and death are bit-players in an overarching projection of cool mastery over the world. But for real soldiers in real wars, death is no joke, no fantasy world: these young men are really scared:

> You don't know who the enemy is.
> It could be a can of Coke or a couple of kids.

These soldiers are grieving the proximity of death, not glorying in their mastery over death. They are grieving having to be terrified of groups of children or roadside litter. This is not bravado. This is the blues.

Developing ideas from Ralph Ellison, music historian Craig Werner describes the blues:

> The blues present a philosophy of life, a three-step process . . . consist[ing] of (1) fingering the jagged grain of your brutal experience; (2) finding a near-tragic, near-comic voice to express that experience; and (3) reaffirming your existence. The first two steps run parallel to [gospel music's] determination to bear witness to the reality of the burden. But where gospel holds out the hope that things will change, that there's a better world coming, the blues settle for making it through the night.

What is a bluesman soldier to do if he is going through the hell of war alone, while many people back home are emotionally incapable of listening to stories of grief and fear? A group called 4th25 (Fourth Quarter) put it this way in a song called "Holding My Breath":

> It's too much for you to feel my pain,
> So I send you all smiles
> Hold my breath telling you it's all right
> The truth is I'm drowning.

They've also dispensed of all projections of control:

There's too much on my shoulders here
And I just can't cope with it, knowing death's around the corner
And I'm standing so close to it
I know I'm supposed to show no emotion,
But it's getting harder to focus because
The reality of my life here is that I have no control of it.

In the midst of the violent imagery of war, Soldier Rap is all about feelings. For a society terrified of pain, denial—via the hardness of cool—may well be the best tool in the emotional toolbox. But compassion pushes us straight **Real compassion** through cool into the arena of pain and suffering. **is not sexy. It is** And when we get there, we find Jesus, the suffering servant. Ridley Usherwood, a pastor and reserve U.S. Air Force chaplain, says: "Many of the **inefficient and** returning soldiers are traumatized in various **painful. And it is** ways and will suffer for a long time. We can't expect them to pick up where they left off. The **also faith, and** church must provide TLC for them. The church **hope, and love.** can help restore them to spiritual health, not just **This is real** mental health." **church.**

Who will go into the places of misery, the places of broken hearts, the places where wounds can't be healed without grisly compassion? Who will have courageous compassion to come alongside the suffering, and to show them in our very bodies the glory of the suffering king? This is real compassion. It is not sexy. It is not cool. It is inefficient and painful. And it is also faith, and hope, and love. This is real church.

LISTENING

A lot of the world's hostility to the church is actually a plea for the church to be the church. It's capricious, to be sure: the world will also ridicule believers no matter how cool we try to be. At the same time, the world desperately wants the church to be authentic and spiritually powerful. The world doesn't want the church to be cool.

Cool Christians often talk about being rebels to the world. Sometimes, the world knows that the church is not living up to our own founder's expectations. Sometimes, God uses nonbelievers to rebuke his church. We should submit to godly rebuke, in whatever package it comes. If all truth is God's truth, there is a lot we can learn from people we don't like. The obstacle is our pride.

The world doesn't want the church to be cool. The world wants a church that has the capacity for compassion.

Neither God nor the world wants a cool Christianity. The world wants a church that has the capacity for compassion. Just as Jesse Jackson invited a numb nation to feel the suffering of the people of New Orleans, so God invites—rather commands—his beloved community to enter into the suffering of real life, carrying nothing but loving compassion.

The world is wide open for the gospel, even the hardest places. It takes real love, through real relationships, over the long haul (which is the only haul that matters). If our Christian witness is not compelling to a suffering world, perhaps it is we who need to be saved. We have to become different people, by the power of God's love transforming our hearts. Hearts transformed over time, soft towards antagonists, submissive to rebuke: that is not cool. But it is real.

8

DEEP UNCOOL

Reconciling the World

Athletic pants rolled across the cobblestones. There was a young man inside them, and when he reached his intended destination, he unfolded himself and sprung into the air, next to four other obviously American kids. They gave each other high fives. A fifth kid stood off to the side, beat-boxing—laying down rhythms for the street drama troupe with no instrument other than his mouth. He was the star of the show, as far as this Swiss audience was concerned. We'd all seen traveling evangelists before. But beat-boxing—that was something new.

The missionaries proceeded to put on a break-dance show concluding with a gospel presentation. One kid tried to engage the spectators like any good American showman, instructing us to give it up for the next kid's moves. The next ten minutes gave us a rapid succession of the latest urban dances from America. Then they broke to rap at us—about Jesus or the Bible or something like that. The main message seemed to be that if we bought into whatever lighthearted and cool Jesus they seemed to read out of the Bible, we too could be lighthearted and cool like them.

It was cool. It was impressive. And that day, even as a sixteen-year-old, I saw cool's built-in limitations as a missional tool. This presentation did not come to bear on local needs, questions or spiritual realities. It felt like a blast from somewhere so far out of the known world that these missionaries might as well have been inviting us to join a circus.

When people are bound by chains of sin and despair, they need someone to get off the cool train and get to know them, their stories, their issues and the reasons they live like they do. They need preachers who will speak the truth out of a sense of compassion.

Nearly everyone around the world is initially attracted to cool. Set up some cool presentation on some street nearly anywhere in the world, and you will get an audience. But an audience alone does not make for authentic proclamation of the gospel, and cool does not equal relevance. Sure, people want to be cool. But when people are all alone like lost sheep, when they need love and community, cool has little missionary power.

DEEP STORIES

When I ran into this street theater, I was walking with my friends down Niederdorf, the hippest street in Zurich. This cobblestone street had artisan carpentry shops and watch repair shops, along with radical bookstores, esoteric and mystical institutes, and the world-famous "Condomeria," for all your prophylactic needs. Sprüngli, the finest chocolate store in the universe, is on Niederdorf, as are diverse pastry shops, beer joints and ornate little fountains. On Niederdorf, Switzerland is on display, in all its glory and lostness.

In one sense Niederdorf was a logical choice for a presentation, with its smallish squares where crowds could easily be assembled. The main problem with these missionaries was context. I am certain they had put on the same presentation all across central Europe. They had no idea where they were. They had no sense of the weight of place.

There was another street preacher on Niederdorf a while back— five centuries back. Ulrich Zwingli, cofounder of the Protestant Reformation, began his career right on this street. Zwingli taught a contextualized gospel to a Swiss audience and had a profound impact on the city's spiritual life. Anyone who wishes to reach Zurich for Christ must first understand that Zurich has been reached for Christ for a long, long time.

Cabaret Voltaire may have looked like any other raunchy nightclub to visiting missionaries, but in addition to being an active bar, it was the origin of the surrealist Dada movement in the arts. World War I had thrown Europe into such an existential and spiritual crisis that absurdity and surrealism had seemed like the only answer. Dada's anti-art predated by seventy years Sprite's anti-advertising advertisements. It all started here on Niederdorf.

Karl Jung, the philosopher/psychologist who brought spiritualism into psychology, used to walk this street. So did James Joyce (who is buried nearby), Richard Wagner, Albert Einstein, Benito Mussolini and others. Vladimir Lenin prepared the Russian revolution from Café Odeon, one block off Niederdorf.

For a quintessentially European-looking street, Niederdorf's paving stones were relatively new—they had only in place since the late 1940s. During World War II, when Nazi armies surrounded landlocked Switzerland, and hunger and fear had been a constant reality, most of Zurich's open spaces had been torn up to plant potatoes. Rooftops had wheat crops growing on them. Even in wealthy Switzerland, fear of starvation sticks, even in the inherited memories of those born much later. Every local, even cool-inclined teenagers, carries the memory to some degree or another as they walk through that street.

Questions of the profoundest sort have been asked on this street, and still echo between Niederdorf's crowded buildings: *What is true? Why is life better than death? What now after all this insanity? Can the soul be rebuilt without God? Does any of this mean anything at all?* These are real questions, not just topics for late-night conversation. People commit suicide over these questions.

In a place like Niederdorf, in a place where God is dead, where the steep cliffs of the valley of the shadow of death close in around the soul, cool is not just a bad vehicle for announcing God's reign. It is teaching starving people some fine dance moves: it makes a mockery of their hunger. Where there is existential despair, apologetics alone won't cut it. Neither will a hip, cool Jesus.

Cool is teaching starving people some fine dance moves: it makes a mockery of their hunger.

It doesn't matter how much of a crowd will gather for a cool show. It doesn't matter how rebellious we make Jesus out to be. People need a Jesus who can confront history's horrors; they need a Jesus relevant to place.

The world is big, endlessly complicated, stunningly beautiful and heart-breakingly bitter. And wherever we go, from our campuses to our neighborhoods, we must remember that if God is dead for so many locals, it is not necessarily because the gospel has never been preached. Sometimes different answers are needed, and cool Christianity is rarely the right one.

LISTEN TO THE STORIES

When it comes to memory, especially the memory of pain, in places like war-torn Europe there still is no generational identity gap. The Swiss teenagers of my youth, who couldn't care less about the story behind Niederdorf's architecture, nevertheless had a solid grasp of history's weight. Born decades after World War II, they inherited, and even passed on to foreigners like me, a memory of the war's horrors. As children involved in the Boy Scouts, for instance, we didn't wear scout uniforms (like the rest of the world's troops) because of their inevitable association with Nazi youth brigades. To this day I have to force myself not to panic at hip hop concerts, when rappers make the entire audience raise their right hands in the air. I can almost hear "Heil Hitler!"

Memory lasts, but a cool gospel doesn't. Absent deeply communal understanding, we expect to relate to other people simply as individuals wherever we go. It's doubtful that those American street performers back in Zurich understood the weight of American realities on their mission. In the 1980s, Ronald Reagan had placed intercontinental ballistic missiles carrying nuclear warheads at American military installations across Western Europe. To Reagan and to most Americans, it was a strategic ploy to prod the Soviets into an arms race they couldn't afford. Europeans were terrified to have suddenly become a target in an intergalactic battle. For Reagan, it seemed, Europeans existed as nothing more than a buffer between America and Russia. In the end, Reagan's strategy worked, and the Soviet Union collapsed. But so did European faith in American goodness. In a game of brinkmanship, Reagan was the cowboy who dared the villain to shoot a civilian.

We live in social realities, whether we like it or not, as part of a complicated and dynamic historical process. America is part of history, and America has a history, and more important, in the eyes of the world Americans themselves are intrinsically implicated in American history. And we are not liberated from the weight of history just because we didn't support such-and-such a policy or political candidate.

BELOVED COMMUNITY AND RELIGION

The church won't be free from the burden of history until we get to heaven. But until then God demands, and the Holy Spirit empowers, life together as one, holy, universal church—as a beloved community.

In fact, the church is the only community that will last. It is an international, multilingual and multitribal organic body, whose very existence is the greatest witness Christians will ever be able to muster. God through the Holy Spirit is creating *a community* called the church, with whom he will live forever in fellowship. The church is created in God's image just as its constituent individuals are in their own right. The church is a living critter.

Life together is about digging deep into each other's lives and sorrows. Left unguarded, the very source of evangelical strength, an emphasis on *personal* faith, can veer into *private* faith—cool faith. Evangelicals should learn to practice community in worship. We are not just a collection of people, a "club saved," but a foretaste of eternity.

The cool world abhors tradition but longs for the lost weight of transcendent rituals.

The lost are invited into intimate and vulnerable participation in the community created by the Holy Spirit. Cool loses all attractiveness next to the stuff of real and abundant life in Christ. In the long run, the real world is the church.

God has created in the church the world's most international body. African, Asian and Latin American believers—who make up the majority of the contemporary church—are building up the church among the poor and suffering. They are wasting away in prison for the sake of the gospel. They are developing the most new applications of the gospel for daily life. They often make no bones about being "religious" because they understand that tradition—rituals and even spiritual exercises done by rote—has a proper place in the spirit-filled life.

Tradition is a bad word for those of us who have been hurt by it, but at its best tradition connects us to the saints who have gone before us. The bulk of what we do in life we do by rote. How many times have you shaken someone's hand without giving much thought to the actual choreography of it? What keeps us from getting tripped up on the physical motion of the handshake is the rote nature of it. Handshaking is a greeting ritual. And like the best rituals, we are usually so rehearsed in handshaking that we can use it to communicate the greeting. When rituals link us to tradition, especially when they are familiar enough for us to see through the motions, they are visible reminders of the transcendent.

The cool world abhors tradition but longs for the lost weight of transcendent rituals. So the cool world invents rituals and traditions—festivals like Burning Man, the annual bacchanal in the Nevada desert; sacramental spaces like the altar-like DJ station at a rave; even insider codes of ethics for graffiti writers. Rituals are part of what makes us human, but they are so much deeper and richer when we can connect them to the deep past.

In fact, church history is a great asset as we seek to engage a world hungry for ritual. All too often, however, we hate what's most beautiful about us. Thus a Florida Bible school advertises proudly, "Finally a Bible College that Defies Religion!" Cool Christianity is all too often a performance tailored toward insider consumers; meanwhile, the world wants the church to be the church.

Let's face it: Christian faith is a religion, a living faith that has been handed down through the ages. For well over a millennium, for instance, the church has marked the Lenten period (the forty days leading up to Easter) with extraordinary fasting and prayer. Fasting for Lent is not prescribed in Scripture, but fasting itself has plenty of scriptural precedence. As individuals, our fasting is about each of us and God, and when we fast together with other believers, our hunger connects us to the spiritual life of God's body. It makes good practical and spiritual sense to join the discipline of fasting with the observation of Christ's suffering and resurrection. Likewise, when we receive Communion, we explicitly share fellowship with Christ's suffering as a global community. Wherever we receive bread and wine—on a hospital bed or a battlefield—the Eucharist connects us across the world and across the ages to millions of saints sharing in Christ's life together. Christianity is a religion, and the Holy Spirit is alive and well there.

FORGIVENESS

No human structure will ever be able to come close to the reconciliation possible in Christ. When it comes to justice and mercy, the beloved community has a leg up on the world. We don't have to worry about

who is first, because we're a monarchy under Jesus. We don't have to
worry about who is last, because our king tells us the last will be first.
Our king doesn't have us negotiate with one another; he has us love one
another, be patient with one another and serve one another. Jesus
doesn't even allow us pettiness: Paul pleads with two disputing church
members to "be of one mind in the Lord" (Philippians 4:2).

In God's economy, that magical economy where love creates
more love, we forgive and forgive and forgive. We pour ourselves
out, because Christ's love is big enough to keep us full. We give and
we receive. We grow ever less independent. We don't have to protect ourselves. And we become more vulnerable with each other
where it counts. Our destination isn't treaties, signed across a negotiating table; our destination is family, sharing life together
around a kitchen table.

Crosscultural faith is a beautiful thing, but with crosscultural intimacy comes crosscultural pain. Such pain comes more out of stupidity than malice, which doesn't make it hurt any less. I've been living
in a multiracial church community long enough to have had my share
of hurts, meltdowns and blowups. All the while, however, I've also
grown far thirstier for resolution, because I want more than to survive. I want deep peace and belonging in my church. I don't want to
stay out on the porch. That's where we leave strangers. Nor do I want
to stay seated at the dining room table. That's where we leave honored
guests. No, I want into the kitchen, where real family lives.

There will always be hurt, so I've had to teach myself a discipline
I've begun calling "preemptive forgiveness": I extend forgiveness in
advance, before any wrong has been done, so that I can love the ignorant perpetrator at the moment of the insult. Jesus once said, "Be care-
ful not to do your 'acts of righteousness' in front of others, to be seen
by them. . . . Do not let your left hand know what your right hand is
doing, so that your giving may be in secret" (Matthew 6:1, 3-4). Preemptive forgiveness is a secret gift to an offender who will never be

able to understand that he or she is offending, and will never know how much she has been given.

Extending forgiveness is much bigger than not pursuing vengeance. To its credit, cool has never been big on vengeance. Cool just pretends life is no big deal. But life *is* a big deal, and relationships are too precious and too important to treat with cool shrugs. We need forgiveness from each other much more than we need "no problem." Forgiveness is a gift to others, but "no big deal" is a gift we give ourselves. We say "no big deal" when we don't want to have a conflict; we forgive as a sign of true understanding.

I am certain that whatever skills of preemptive forgiveness I've learned are second nature to many of my African American friends. As a white person in contemporary society, I get unearned breaks all the time—from extra courtesy at the store, to easier access to justice. It's not fair that others have to work twice as hard as me to get to the same place. For them, Christian living is one long journey in forgiveness.

THE REAL REVOLUTION

Preemptive forgiveness is only half the story, however, because without confronting deep-seated evils, reconciliation is cheap and even phony. We have to really hear each other's stories.

Sometimes you need an outsider's perspective. Western Christians are far more adjusted to individualism, rebellion, consumerism and cynicism than most of the world's believers. If we are ever going to learn to hear God's voice in new and surprising ways, we'll first have to develop the skill of listening to the stories of people unlike ourselves, including those who hate God and the gospel. Really listening is the difference between humane compassion on the one hand, and cool voyeurism on the other.

The fact of the matter is that we have much to learn from unbelievers. Sometimes mere exposure to dissenting ideas is enough to help us understand why we believe at all. While I was in college I made it

a hobby to go hear guest lectures from visiting professors. The further
away from my beliefs the better. During my anti-globalism activist
phase I listened to a lecture by Mexico's trade secretary and learned to
distinguish global capitalism from its abuses; I learned that most of
the injustices in international trade are flat-out illegal. I learned that
the trick to justice is not hobbling corporations but enforcing laws already on the books.

On another night I went to an eye-opening lecture by a lesbian
philosopher titled "The Case Against Marriage." It was a discussion
within the gay community about the political strategy of pushing for
gay marriage. The politics were familiar, but what really caused me to
think was this philosopher's philosophy of gender. I learned to re-
think a lot of what I unthinkingly "knew" about male and female (and
the significance of that line in Genesis 1:27). More important, I
gained an insight into the fundamental worldviews behind most political debates about homosexuality.

Over the years I've heard lectures on disposable diapers, punctu-
ated equilibrium in evolution, Tibetan communism, female circumci-
sion in Africa, the politics of the Olympic Games and the effects of in-
breeding on dairy cattle. Most of these have had no impact on my
faith, but have made me a healthier soul overall: I've learned to listen
to new ideas. Meanwhile, listening to occasional lectures by vehe-
mently anti-Christian thinkers has been very good for my faith.

But the biggest surprises have come when I've entered a lecture
hall with prejudices. One such moment, during my freshman year in
college, shook the foundations of my faith. A major African American
public intellectual spoke on racism, and I wanted to go precisely because I wanted to be offended. I did not expect to be confronted with
the gospel. Even less did I expect to be shown the yawning chasm between Scripture and the latent white-supremacy lingering in the faith
I had learned at the evangelical churches of my youth.

The Reverend Cornel West is a liberal in most senses of the word, but he hadn't come to talk about politics like I'd expected. He came to talk about our hearts. He came assuming a white audience in need of salvation. I was part of that audience in need of salvation. My faith has never been the same since. That was the day I began to care about race in America.

Eventually several white friends and I decided to join the church that has become our home. It has been a long journey, these last nine years. I grew really close to my white friends and comembers of my church. (One of them eventually agreed to marry me!) In fact, none of us would have been able to preserve our hearts without a little bit of white space in a largely black church community. We've been lonely at times, and angry as hornets at others. But over the long haul, our church has become our home. Our African American family has become part of who we are.

Church is messy and difficult, just like any family. The church is about more than tolerance. The church is about love. The church is the most revolutionary force in world history. But the revolution will go unnoticed except in hindsight: the Holy Spirit creating a beloved community.

9

BEYOND COOL

Inherit the Earth

Nothing communicates hope in despair quite like a tree growing on a slag pile. There are many sites of industrial pollution across the Great Lakes, from Minnesota's iron mines to Chicago's steel mills to Flint's stamping plants to Cleveland's oil refineries. From rocks in the ground to gas-guzzling automobiles to road trips: each step along the way leaves behind hundreds of acres of toxic wastelands.

But the Great Lakes region's natural environment dominates even industry. The region gets lots of rain, lots of wind, and above all, has a highly seasonal climate. Bitter cold winters follow sweltering summers. During my first winter in Wisconsin, I actually had ice form on the surface of my eyeball. That's cold.

Flora and fauna in the Great Lakes region are uniquely built to survive such conditions. And if you bundle up tight, and venture out into the frozen prairies and forests, you'll find that it's not as dead as it looks at first glance. In fact, this place is a riot of life. Plants and animals more than survive around here: they prosper.

In Idaho, you can still follow the wagon ruts of Oregon-bound migrants crossing the state in the 1850s. That's how fragile the high desert is. But in the Great Lakes region, plant life is so aggressive that even slag piles will get colonized. Leave a toxic, lifeless heap alone for a few years, and trees begin to grow on top of it. They will never be as strong or successful as trees in the forest, because of all the poisons in their structures, and the lack of nutrients in the slag. In that respect, a tree growing on a slag pile is a tragedy. The tree will never reach its potential, all because we have dumped our industrial waste. But looked at another way, when a tree colonizes a dump, we see an image of the hope Christ gives us. No wasteland is too wasted to turn beautiful. Where we with our finite vision see only deadness, God sees potential. Where we see only the waste and the shame of our past hurts, God sees the beginning of his reign. Jesus' vision extends far beyond the deadness around us:

> Blessed are the poor in spirit,
>   for theirs is the kingdom of heaven.
> Blessed are those who mourn,
>   for they will be comforted.
> Blessed are the meek,
>   for they will inherit the earth.
> Blessed are those who hunger and thirst for righteousness,
>   for they will be filled. (Matthew 5:3-6)

War, injustice, poverty, eating disorders, bullies and broken family relationships: someday this will all be a distant memory. God is coming for his people, and is moving in the church by the power of his Spirit. God is making new life spring up like trees on a slag pile, like a child born in a refugee camp. If we look closely enough, we can see God creating life in the presence of so much death.

I conclude this book with a vision of what life could be like. Life beyond cool could be about love and community and belonging and spiritual fruit.

OUR HOPE

Cool asks a very important question that demands an answer from the church: Why would anyone want to inherit the earth? If the world is nothing but a slag pile, what good does it do to stop being cool? People aren't fools. There is a good reason they choose to live for the moment: they have no hope beyond the moment.

Cool sees its cynical attitude as authentic and superior to the sweetness of love. But cool's vision is limited; it can only see the stunted tree on the slag pile. Cool never sees the miracle of quiet healing. The world we are about to inherit is profoundly sweet. God is going to tear down any obstacle to our loving each other. This reign of love is so much more authentic than cool's huffy "keeping it real." And this love will last.

In his letter to the Ephesians, Paul said:

> I pray that the eyes of your heart may be enlightened in order that you may know the hope to which he has called you, the riches of his glorious inheritance in his people, and his incomparably great power for us who believe (Ephesians 1:18-19).

Paul wants us to know about something we don't see with our eyes: our inheritance. We are going to inherit the earth one day—not conquer the earth, but inherit it as a gift from God. God is taking us somewhere big. By the power of his love, we can do more than merely *transgress* cool with anti-cool or *uncool*; instead love lets us *transcend* cool altogether.

Our Christian hope is anchored in the real world, not in some mystical nirvana. Missionary and author Bob Morris explains:

> Children of the Kingdom must see the greater reality of the unseen, and Paul prays that we will be enlightened specifically to see three eternal realities—the hope to which he has called us, and the riches of his glorious inheritance in the saints, and his incomparably great power.

Christian hope is thus "hipi" in the true sense of the word—seeing farther, seeing beyond.Christian hope is *hip* because it opens our eyes to the real deal. But the world is not hip to the realities of eternity. To a world with no hope, Christian hope is pure fantasy or opiate. Morris continues:

> "Hope" in common English usage means something less than Biblical hope. We may hope to win the lottery or hope it doesn't rain, but it is a very different kind of hope to which God has called us. The writer to the Hebrews puts it this way: "Faith is being sure of what we hope for and certain of what we do not see." There is no sense here of "hoping against hope" or of fantasy. As William Barclay says, "[Christian hope] is not simply a trembling hesitant hope that perhaps the promises of God may be true. It is the confident expectation that they cannot be anything else than true." That is the robust hope that Paul prays we will know.

It is no accident that cool emerged in slavery: cool's living for the moment is an explicit rejection of hope in a hopeless situation. Cool hopelessness is an attitude people adopt as a last-ditch effort to exert some control over an absolutely uncontrollable situation. It is furthermore no accident that cool went mainstream after the dawn of nuclear warfare. Norman Mailer set the birth of white cool at Hiroshima:

> [Today's humans] live with the suppressed knowledge that the smallest facets of our personality or the most minor projection of our ideas, or indeed the absence of personality could mean equally well that we might be doomed to die as a cipher in some vast statistical operation in which our teeth might be counted, and our hair would be saved, but our death itself would be unknown, unhonored, and unremarked, a death which could not follow with dignity as a possible consequence of serious actions we had chosen.

The end of Stanley Kubrick's film about nuclear holocaust, *Dr. Strangelove, Or: How I Learned to Stop Worrying and Love the Bomb,* shows city after city being vaporized in an instant, to the soundtrack of a beautiful song about friendship. The ballet of destruction begins with a cowboy falling out of the sky on top of a bomb. In the face of the instantaneous and anonymous death awaiting him as soon as he hits the ground, the cowboy rides the bomb like a bucking bronco, howling out with his dying breath an incredible "yee-haw." It's the most hauntingly sick joke I've ever seen on film. But if the world is indeed going to hell, the best we can hope for is a sick joke.

Even without the threat of nuclear holocaust, life can lose its meaning. Today, especially around the holidays, it can feel like we live in a bleak commercial landscape of hypnotizing shopping malls big enough to warrant their own off-ramps from clogged expressways. We live in a world where movies are test-marketed for global audiences, and local flavors are rejected in favor of bland uniformity. When culture is for sale, is there any better response than becoming bored cynics?

Against such a backdrop, only a transcendent hope will do—and that is precisely the hope we have in Christ.

STIRRING THE MEMORY POT

The safe blandness of our commercial society only reflects the safe blandness of our own hearts: we have forgotten how to remember the past. Many of us are heirs of a multigenerational project, begun at border crossings and ports of entry, of strategic forgetfulness.

The history of North America is the history of immigration. People from every nation in the world have begun new lives on these shores. For most immigrants, the New World was a dash of hope against a horrid situation. Some were driven from their homes by famine and poverty; others came because of injustice, ethnic cleansing and religious persecution.

Many arrived illiterate, and some, coming from minority groups in their own countries, were even unable to speak the official languages of their homelands. Many carried bigger burdens in shame and trauma than they carried clothes on their backs. And many vowed, upon reaching these shores, to dispense of all their painful memories from the Old World. They cut out their past and their culture, speaking only English with their children.

Immigration always involves loss. Garrison Keillor's fictional account of Norwegian farmers in Minnesota describes the loss of home:

> America was the land where they were old and sick, Norway where they were young and full of hopes—and much smarter, for you are never so smart again in a language learned in middle age nor so romantic or brave or kind. All the best of you is in the old tongue, but when you speak your best in America you become a yokel, a dumb Norskie, and when you speak English, an idiot.

Today's immigrants from Asia, Africa and Latin America experience the same loss in different contexts. The trauma of immigration is the loss of culture. Where the first generation fails to assimilate, their children don't like getting made to feel ashamed of their ethnic peculiarity ("She goes to that weird church" . . . "What is that in your lunchbox?"), so they try to bury their roots. By the third and fourth generation, a thousand years of cultural memory may be dead.

This loss is what white people are trying to express with the claim, in interracial conversations, not to have any culture. Nonwhite people are invariably astonished or angered to hear such claims; they have the advantage of an outsider's perspective. To them it seems as obvious as light of day that white people have a distinct culture. And for years, I repeated that line in conversations about race, trying to convince whites that the feelings they have of rootlessness are nothing more than feelings; all they need to do is look around themselves to see that they have culture.

But lately I've realized that white cultural homelessness is real. When white people complain of not having ethnicity, they are expressing the pain of their grandparents' decisions to throw away ethnicity. Immigrant families felt that their ethnicity was shameful and needed to be hidden. They also knew that in an intensely racialized society, becoming white was the best way to ensure opportunities for their children. Today their descendents feel the loneliness of having no culture. For white people of this generation then, part of the spiritual work of bringing God's healing is to stir the pot of family memory. Ask your grandparents and parents about their ethnic memories. If your family descends from involuntary (slave) immigrants, ask around about family stories and rituals. See what emotions begin to float around in the family. Bring God's validation of culture into the conversation. This is the work of restoration. This is the work of healing. This is deep work, and it becomes possible when we move beyond cool to compassion.

My town, Madison, is perhaps the only city in Wisconsin with any chance at being considered a worldly, sophisticated place. Milwaukee is too blue collar, and Green Bay is right out: any city in which wearing cheese on one's head is a fashion statement doesn't stand a chance. Madison, however, has the University of Wisconsin, the state capitol, and the best art museums, theaters and performance spaces between Chicago and Minneapolis.

Madison is also incredibly paranoid about becoming Milwaukee or Green Bay. God forbid the working classes in Madison start to party according to working class tastes! To safeguard Madison's cool, the city boosters sponsor art fairs and free operas in city parks.

In the 1870s, German, Polish and Irish immigrants flooded the state. Milwaukee was utterly transformed into the brilliantly multiethnic community it is today. Long after most European immigrants to the United States assimilated into bland whiteness, having given away their colorful heritage and smelly foods for a chance at middle-class respectability, Milwaukee continues to pulse with Croatian-singing polka bands, German sausage races and ethnic neighborhoods. And today's Mexican, Hmong and Arab immigrants have settled right in, participating in the cultural show-and-tell that dazzles the eyes. Summer in Milwaukee is one long party, with dozens of ethnic culture and food festivals, from Juneteenth to Oktoberfest; from Indian Summer Days to Arabfest.

Madison, on the other hand, put up a fight in the face of the onslaught of raucous hordes, a fight that continues to this day. At one point, nearly 70 percent of Madison was foreign-born; in the 1870s the city passed laws designed to silence the Germans' oom-pah music and parties that tended to consume entire parks and surrounding neighborhoods. The city elites' respectable aesthetic of colorless minimalism didn't stand a chance in the free-market of culture, so it needed the support of the law.

But the Bible's version of heaven sounds a lot more like Milwaukee's than Madison's (although it's a good bet that heaven will not contain Milwaukee's industrial pollution and segregation policies). Heaven will be very colorful indeed, with intensely smelly food and even oom-pah music. The book of Revelation describes the New Jerusalem God will create one day:

> On no day will [the New Jerusalem's] gates ever be shut. . . . The glory and honor of the nations will be brought into it. (Revelation 21:25-26)

Our Christian hope lies in a brilliant future, a future where the nations will retain their glory. And furthermore, since prowess in warfare won't be highly valued in heaven (we'll have beaten our swords into plowshares, after all), "the honor and glory of the nations" will consist of culture, beauty, joy, cooking, dancing and singing and telling the stories of God's faithfulness towards our own respective nations.

The work of redeemed memory and redeemed culture is part of worship. When we restore what was buried out of shame, and present it to the church as an expression of new life, we are tasting heaven's first fruits.

God created us in his image. That image has always proven irrepressible, even among the lost. Just as God's creation, when it does what he made it to do, can colonize even chemical dumps, we should not be surprised to discover hairline cracks in the phony and boring façade—cultural trees, as it were, sprouting out of the slag pile of cool.

RUINING THE PAVEMENT

There is another industrial wreck I have been watching for some years now: an abandoned munitions plant not far from Madison. During World War II, three shifts of workers built the bullets and bombs that defeated Hitler. Badger Munitions Plant was decommissioned a while back, and the plant's thousands of acres are currently the subject of complex negotiations. Some want to restore the land to the families of the farmers who made way for the factory sixty years ago. The local Ho-Chunk Indian Nation has a legitimate claim to the land and is participating in the dialogue. Others point to the large state park immediately north of the plant and suggest the state annex the plant and restore it to tall-grass prairie.

Ever since negotiations started ten years ago, the Army has stopped maintaining most of the plant. So while the interested parties have yet to arrive on an agreement, outsiders like me have witnessed a gentle transformation take place: The parking lot has become a prairie once again, without any human help.

At first it was just grass poking through the cracks. But left untended, grass has the power to shatter the pavement. With each passing year, more cracks appeared, and more grasses appeared to fill them, and the process has accelerated. Grass captures water, preventing runoff and flashfloods downstream. Instead the water is absorbed into the soil, regenerating underground life, like worms and such. And those worms in turn begin the slow process of restoring the soil to its original prosperity.

Far more than mere grass, tall-grass prairie contains more biodiversity than any other ecological zone in North America save rainforests. But what really makes the prairie grand is the underground life. It's the fungi, grubs and roots that combine to make the prairie fertile. When pioneer grass plants shatter the pavement, it's an expression of the pavement's failure to sufficiently bury what was going on underneath. But once the soil is able to create some above-ground breathing room for itself, restoration kicks into high gear. And it all started with a little crack in the pavement.

The cracks in cool's façade have always been there. Cool contains too many contradictions, and has not been able to conquer every corner.

Craig Van Gelder's *The Essence of the Church* contains a great image for the church: God's demonstration plot. For folk without an agricultural background, a demonstration plot is a piece of land used by researchers and state agriculture agents to prove new farming methods and seeds. Each year, Van Gelder writes,

> A strip of land, usually along a major roadway, was selected as a demonstration plot, where a new farming method, seed, or fertilizer was used to raise a crop. It was not uncommon for farmers to remain skeptical throughout the summer as crops grew. But there was always keen interest in the fall when the crop was harvested. Invariably the innovation performed better than the crops in the surrounding fields. By the next year, many farmers, including my dad, would be using the innovation as if it had been their idea all along.

The church is God's demonstration plot in the world. Its very existence demonstrates that his redemptive reign has already begun. Its very presence invites the world to watch, listen, examine and consider accepting God's reign as a superior way of living.

Until the day comes when God will settle all disputes, we the church will be God's living demonstration of what life could be like. We the church are a foretaste of heaven, because like in heaven, when the church is living as it should, no one makes us afraid any more. We don't have to protect ourselves.

In Micah's Old Testament vision of God's healing for the nations, "in the last days," we find a depiction of lasting peace between communities:

> [The LORD] will judge between many peoples
>   and will settle disputes for strong nations far and wide.
> They will beat their swords into plowshares
>   and their spears into pruning hooks.
> Nation will not take up sword against nation,
>   nor will they train for war anymore.
> Everyone will sit under their own vine
>   and under their own fig tree,
> and no one will make them afraid,
>   for the LORD Almighty has spoken. (Micah 4:3-4)

Whatever peace we have begins with God. He will resolve humanly irresolvable conflicts. And he does it not by the authority of international treaties or other pieces of paper, but by his own authority. (To make sure we don't miss the point that this reconciliation is not manmade, God is explicit: "for the LORD Almighty has spoken.")

SHAMELESS AUTHENTICITY

During my adolescent years, right at the time when we moved from Switzerland to the United States, my father taught me a lesson about life that has influenced nearly all of my subsequent interactions with people. It was about approaching other cultures with curiosity.

We didn't know where in the United States we were headed: a lot depended on my dad's employment. Some leading candidates included Dallas and Denver. I looked up maps and books on both places, learning what I could. Both are perennial boomtowns, full of people with big dreams and big shoulders. Denver had the mountains; Dallas the hot weather. And both were exploding with entertainment.

But it was not to be. Wisconsin won out. I put on an immature attitude. "There's nothing to do in Wisconsin," I believe I said. This much I knew: Wisconsin is cold, and it has cheese. As it turned out, I was correct on both accounts. Had I known more about the stereotypes, I could have added that there is polka music in Wisconsin, and people spend much of their lives dreaming about fishing, talking about the weather, and thinking about the Green Bay Packers.

My father gave me a few days to simmer down before replying. "Wherever in the world you go," he said, "you will find people who live there for a reason. When we move, your job will be to learn *why* people live there." Thus in one little sentence, my father opened my heart to seeing the world through gently curious eyes.

During my family's first month in Madison, I was exploring the radio dial, and landed on a classic rock station. Nearly everything was new to me, from the music itself to the inane banter of the disc jockeys. A station identification spot cracked me up. "Rocking America's Dairyland," a tough guy's voice announced, followed by the sound of a cow mooing, interrupted by a heavy metal guitar lick.

I considered my father's challenge: *Find out why they live there.* "People live here," I concluded, "because they can't easily move to a cool place, like Dallas or Denver. But they're determined to make the best of it. They're rocking America's Dairyland. Cows aren't cool; they're saying 'We may only be a Dairyland, but we rock nonetheless.'"

If that line of reasoning made sense to me at the time, I couldn't have been more wrong. There is something far worse going on in this culture (from the vantage point of cool): an awful lot of people in Wisconsin actually think cheese and cows are cool. That's why a crowd of Wisconsinite fans at national sporting events always includes some soul with a foam wedge of cheese on his head: if Cheeseheads were just a joke or a novelty, it would have worn off years ago. When WIBA boasted of rocking America's Dairyland, the clip of the cow was there to bolster the claim: this state is a rocking state, and this radio station is the center of it all.

There was no irony and no shame involved in the Dairyland boast: Wisconsinites are passionate about their dairy. They think hunting is cool. Many even think polka is cool. The Packers are certainly cool. Wisconsin is a place unashamed of its peasant roots. They like cheese, and like the rest of us, they want to be cool.

One reason we rarely sing recreationally anymore is because we're afraid of looking uncool, too sincere. But singing is authentically expressive. When we let down our guard and indulge in some shameless singing, we usually feel the better for it. A lot of the reason for worship music's revival in popular church culture has to do with a generation of young Christians deciding to sing together. Singing touches the heart, and authenticity can be communicated through song. And in a group, no one needs to know that you're tone-deaf.

The Swiss love to sing. They've got hiking songs, and morning and evening songs, and prayer songs. They've got company songs, courting songs, songs to cheer on their soccer teams, and story songs. And, of course, they've got all range of whimsical mouth noise songs, the most famous of which are yodels. In that no-nonsense culture, singing is one of the preferred avenues for laughter and exuberance. The Swiss rarely sing to perform; they sing to share their feelings and their real selves. Singing, for the Swiss, is very deep, very real and vulnerable. It's simultaneously a gift, a pleasure and a seal of fellowship.

Singing, in the Swiss sense, is thus profoundly uncool.

One of the distinguishing marks of black Pentecostal churches, similarly, is their unashamed preservation of some of the musical heritage of slavery and poverty. "Whooping," "tuning up," "lining-out" and "shouting" are all musical or rhythmic forms of expression African Americans developed early in their church history. In addition to bringing African tonal, call-and-response and polyrhythmic sensibilities into the church, African American slaves heard the gospel and understood its power to transcend culture and social structures alike. They furthermore understood the subversive message of the gospel, with the dignity, supernatural perception and spiritual fruit it gives to those who believe. The gospel gave sight to the blind, healing from sins and from demonic oppression, and pronounced adoption into the king's very family. This contextualized gospel was life-giving in a life-denying situation. It freed slaves, and later poor African Americans, from feeling ashamed of poverty and segregation.

Over the decades of freedom and a rise in material circumstances, the black church diversified, reaching people of all social classes. Many black churches made, and continue to make, great efforts to gain mainstream respectability by paring away all aspects of slave religion from their liturgies and worship.

But at the lower end of the socio-economic totem pole, Pentecostals have always included the cry of the poor into the strains of worship. Alex Gee, author of *Jesus and the Hip-Hop Prophets* (and my pastor), is a student of the African American church tradition. "Messiness in worship wasn't a black Pentecostal thing," he says. "Worship in a sinful and suffering world, from the Old Testament sacrifices to this day, will always be untidy. But black Pentecostals' innovation was to care more about seeking God's face than saving face in worship. This is why they were able to celebrate the way they did."

What outsiders, black and white alike, have condescendingly called *emotionalism* is actually the emotional product of a profoundly theological consideration: God is emotional, and God's interface with creation—including both Jesus' and the Holy Spirit's—is intensely emotional.

Gee continues: "The early Pentecostals understood God's perception of them (like Hagar in Genesis 16:13 when she calls the Lord "the God who sees me"). This understanding of God—that he doesn't discriminate—is what made the gospel appealing and worship an appropriate reaction to this mind-boggling truth."

God gave deep spiritual perception and emotional intelligence to these supposedly low-class and ignorant Christians. Emotions in worship weren't mere accidents. In their humility before the throne, God gave them the emotional intelligence to fearlessly wield their own emotions, and worship the God who sees the suffering of his people. There is nothing cool about crying out to God from the valley of the shadow of death, and it is a witness in humble worship for all of us who desire authentic Christian religion.

There is nothing shameful about song. Next time you feel the urge, but you censor yourself at the last minute, go ahead. Let it go.

HEAVENLY CHEESE

I am convinced that God delights in Wisconsinites' dairy fancy. This is authenticity at its best. When in heaven people bring to the beloved community the "glory and the honor of the nations," Myron Olson, the master cheesemaker, will present for God's glory perhaps the least cool artifact in the world: a stinky cheese. It might smell worse than a corpse, but Limburger sure tastes good.

The human heart never strays very far from the kitchen. If you want to know who people really are, eat their traditional foods with them. Some foods tell a people's stories in themselves; still others remind people of their stories. It is through stories that we can really enjoy each other and know each other and laugh and grieve with each other. By stories I mean everything people have to tell us. Stories include history (objective stories) and culture (tales, festivals, songs and even the mundane details of table manners and attitudes toward time). At the subjective, personal level, stories include our opinions and the ways God has spoken to us and healed us.

Cool is part of our story, but cool also interferes both with the telling and with the hearing of our story. Whenever we listen to each others' stories, our hearing must be driven by love rather than shame; and compassion rather than pity. When your friends laugh at the stories you find most beautiful—you begin to appreciate just how much greater heaven will be than all this.

A beloved community is far deeper than a conglomeration of individuals. Listening to stories is the foundation for reconciliation. When you get down in the dirt and to the messy work of daily life in community—particularly multiethnic, multicultural community—you begin to realize just how radical the church really is.

YODELING UNCOOL

During a party two years ago, a few friends and I got drafted into an "unknown talents" contest. The emcee made us show off stupid human tricks. The woman immediately ahead of me in the line belted out, to tremendous applause, an impression of various barnyard animals, so I knew I had to come up with something good.

But I had been here before. Years earlier, in Switzerland, as a punishment for acting up in class, my music teacher had made me, along with my partners in crime, stand in front of the class and recite the alpine yodel we'd been working on. (Yes, the Swiss teach yodeling in school!)

That afternoon in high school, of course, I didn't appreciate my yodeling workshop. I was wasting an international education on trying to be cool. For several months running, my friends and I had been engaging our music teacher in a puerile battle of wills, and now Dr. Waldhof was punishing us with public humiliation. He picked a complex folk song, the melody of which ranged quite high. His intent, no doubt, was to force us teenage boys, with our cracking voices, to stumble across the tenor-falsetto boundary. He wanted to humiliate us, and we were determined not to let that happen.

Succumbing to stage fright would have meant victory for Dr. Waldhof—out of the question at the time. We were too cool to lose this battle. So I sang the song. I have no idea how well, but I kept my cool. Dr. Waldhof sat me down, and moved to the next misbehaved boy. I gloried in my victory; I had stood my ground. I was cool. It's all about the performance.

Ten years and four thousand miles later, standing at center stage at a party, the memory of that unremarkable incident seemed almost more real than my present situation. And just like that day in high school, I suddenly lost all stage fright. I knew: I was going to yodel this party down.

But a few things were different this time around: my Swiss heritage had grown much more precious to me. Yodeling is silly in all possible contexts, of course, but it can also be a beautiful and childlike song of celebration. This particular yodel was a song about taking a ferry across a lake instead of hiking around it:

Vo Lozärn gäge Weggis Zue
Yohelodi Du Do Yohelodi Du
Brucht mer wäder Strumpf no Schue
Yohelodi Du Do Ho.
Diiri Yohelodi Du; Yohelodi Du Do Yohelodi Du;
Diiri Yohelodi Du Yohelodi Du Do Ho.

(*"If you're going from Lucerne to Weggis, You need neither shoes nor socks."* That and lots of nonsensical syllables.)

As clearly as I remembered my glory moment of teenage defiance, my motives were far healthier this time. It was only a party game; I was defying no one. This was a dare for my nerves. That's what party games are all about: merriment, not humiliation. There was no real risk of failure, so I was free.

"It's been a while since I've yodeled," I said, to which the partiers responded with hilarious uproar. So far so good; I was going to be OK. And just like ten years earlier, I yodeled with all my might. The partiers hollered with laughter and surprise. This was *itetu*—cool in the original African sense of the word: I had performed a challenging task without breaking a sweat.

In a world beyond cool, we are free to explore love and art and innovation and wisdom. We can be childlike. And we can aim high. We can show our stuff. We can embrace our family and our faith. We can become the beloved community we were created to be.

NOTES

Throughout this book I've mentioned artists and historical events many people might not be familiar with. If you're curious to find out more, my sources—plus videos and pictures—are at <http://uncoolbook.blogspot.com/2006/01/source-material.html>.

Chapter One: You Got to Wear Your Sunglasses

Page 14   *Cool is an attitude:* Dick Pountain and David Robins, *Cool Rules: Anatomy of an Attitude* (London: Reaktion, 2000), p. 19.

Page 16   "It is a particular sensation": W. E. B. Du Bois, *The Souls of Black Folk,* in *The Norton Anthology of African American Literature,* ed. Henry Louis Gates Jr. and Nellie McKay (New York: Norton, 1997), p. 615.

Page 17   Poor whites: John Leland, *Hip: The History* (New York: HarperCollins, 2004), p. 19.

Page 17   "Early in the nineteenth century": Kathleen Neal Cleaver, "The Antidemocratic Power of Whiteness," in *Critical White Studies,* ed. Richard Delgado and Jean Stefancic (Philadelphia: Temple University Press, 1997), p. 160.

Page 17   Caused racial tension to intensify: Emily Field Van Tassel, "Only the Law Would Rule Between Us: Antimiscegenation, the Moral Economy of Dependency, and the Debate over Rights After the Civil War," in *Critical White Studies,* ed. Richard Delgado and Jean Stefancic (Philadelphia: Temple University Press, 1997), p. 152.

Page 18   "The ads": Thomas Frank, *The Conquest of Cool: Business Culture, Counterculture, and the Rise of Hip Consumerism* (Chicago: University of Chicago Press, 1997), p. 55.

Page 18   "The basic task": Ibid., p. 90.

Page 18   Cultural observers: Frank, *Conquest of Cool;* see also David Chaney, *Lifestyles* (New York: Routledge, 1996), p. 99.

Page 19   Whereas standards of beauty: See Rolf Reber et al., *Processing Fluency and Aesthetic Pleasure: Is Beauty in the Perceiver's Processing Experience?* (Personality and Social Psychology Review, 2004, Vol. 8, No. 4, 364-382): "Beauty is in the processing experiences of the beholder, but these processing experiences are themselves, in part, a function of objective stimulus properties and the history of the perceiver's encounters with the stimulus. Hence, beauty appears to be 'in the interaction' between the stimulus and the beholder's cognitive and affective processes."

Page 19   Fashion offers: Joan DeJean, *The Essence of Style: How the French Invented High Fashion, Fine Food, Chic Cafés, Style, Sophistication, and Glamour* (New

York: Free Press, 2005), p. 1.

page 19   "Many women today": Pamela Paul, *Pornified: How Pornography Is Trans-forming Our Lives, Our Relationships, and Our Families* (New York: Times Books, 2005), p. 114.

Page 20   The hostile response: Wal-Mart's concession to organics effectively robbed legions of hipsters of their monopoly on cool; rather than being congratulated for this new direction, the chain was met with surprisingly vivid cynicism. Some sample headlines: the blog Gristmill had "Wal-Mart's Organic Bomb" <http://gristmill.grist.org/story/2006/5/12/63314/8910>; Writing on the Wal.net had "Wal-Mart: Home of Cheap (Organic) Crap" <http://thewritingonthewal.net/?p=952>; *New York Times Magazine* titled its story "Mass Natural" (June 4, 2006).

Page 20   "The dark side of cool": Kalle Lasn, *Culture Jam: How to Reverse America's Suicidal Consumer Binge—and Why We Must* (New York: HarperCollins, 1999), pp. xv-xvi, 113.

Page 21   "powerlessness, disconnection and shame": Lasn, *Culture Jam*, p. 141.

Page 22   "Cool is indispensable": Ibid., p. xiii.

Page 22   The trouble is: Douglas Rushkoff, *Coercion: Why We Listen to What "They" Say* (New York: Riverhead, 1999), p. 189.

Page 22   So business thinkers: See Kevin Roberts, *Lovemarks: The Future Beyond Brands* (New York: Powerhouse Books, 2005).

Page 24   The beloved community shatters: The concept of the beloved community informed and empowered Martin Luther King Jr., every weary step of the way. Charles Marsh, *Beloved Community: How Faith Shapes Social Justice, From the Civil Rights Movement to Today* (New York: Basic Books, 2005), p. 6.

Page 24   When we open our hearts: Ray Aldred, *Cross-Cultural Conversion*, speech delivered at InterVarsity's Urbana 03 convention, published at <www.urbana.org/u2003.session.segment.cfm?segment=48&session=5&ItemTypeID=1>.

Chapter Two: Rebellion on Stage

Page 26   "It is basically via a mood": Lars Svendsen, *A Philosophy of Boredom* (London: Reaktion, 2005), p.111.

Page 27   There are two distinct Ché Guevaras: See Héctor Tobar, *Translation Nation: Defining a New American Identity in the Spanish-Speaking United States* (New York: Riverhead, 2005), p. 3.

Page 30   "the emancipation of the present tense": John Leland, *Hip: The History* (New York: HarperCollins, 2004), p. 42.

Page 30   "paradoxically": Steven Keillor, *This Rebellious House: American History & the Truth of Christianity* (Downers Grove, Ill.: InterVarsity Press, 1996), p. 37.

Page 30   "modern Cool may represent": Pountain and Robins, *Cool Rules*, p. 35.

Page 31   "Cool or *itetu*": Robert Farris Thompson, quoted in Dick Pountain and

David Robins, *Cool Rules: Anatomy of an Attitude* (London: Reaktion, 2000), pp. 35-36.

Page 31   "Cool afforded": Ibid., p. 38.

Page 31   "From the start": Leland, *Hip: The History*, pp. 6-7.

Page 32   "The time has come": James Baldwin, *A Stranger in the Village*, in *The Norton Anthology of African American Literature*, ed. Henry Louis Gates Jr. and Nellie McKay (New York: Norton & Co., 1997), p. 1679.

Page 33   John Leland locates: Leland, *Hip: The History*, pp. 47-48.

Page 33   "The Second World War": Norman Mailer, "The White Negro," IV *Dissent* (Spring 1957), reprinted online by the University of Virginia <http://xroads.virginia.edu/~DRBR2/whitenegro.html>.

Page 34   "[Acedia] contains a rejection of": Lars Svendsen, *A Philosophy of Boredom* (London: Reaktion, 2005), pp. 50-52.

Page 35   "subverts false identities": Mark Medley, "Discovering Our True Identity," *Christian Reflection* 9 (2003): 35.

Chapter Three: The Caucasian Storms Harlem

Page 37   Even as Katrina: "The Shaming of America," *Economist*, September 10, 2005.

Page 39   "I heard the voice of Jesus": Charles Marsh, *Beloved Community: How Faith Shapes Social Justice, From the Civil Rights Movement to Today* (New York: Basic Books, 2005), pp. 31-32.

Page 40   "These Christian kids": Dolphus Weary, quoted in Edward Gilbreath, "Catching Up with a Dream," *Christianity Today*, March 2, 1998.

Page 41   "For those of us" Tom Skinner, *The U.S. Racial Crisis and World Evangelism*, speech delivered at Urbana 70 and published at <www.urbana.org/_articles.cfm?RecordId=185>.

Page 42   "a radical reordering": Larry Neal, *The Black Arts Movement* (1968), in *The Norton Anthology of African American Literature*, ed. Henry Louis Gates Jr. and Nellie McKay (New York: Norton & Co., 1997), p. 1960.

Page 42   "Hip hop has rejected": Todd Boyd, *The New H.N.I.C.: The Death of Civil Rights and the Reign of Hip Hop* (New York: New York University Press, 2002), p. xxi.

Page 43   One white boy from California: Melvin Gibbs, *ThugGods: Spiritual Darkness and Hip-Hop*, in Tate, *Everything but the Burden*, pp. 81-98.

Page 44   White fascination with blackness: Damali Ayo, *How to Rent a Negro* (Chicago: Lawrence Hill Books, 2005), p. 27.

Page 44   white fans of hip hop: Bakari Kitwana, *Why White Kids Love Hip Hop* (New York: Basic Civitas Books, 2005), p. 28.

Page 45   "Black men dealing with their childhoods": bell hooks, *We Real Cool: Black Men and Masculinity* (New York: Routledge, 2004), p. 144.

Page 46   "Is this [white] interest": Rudolph Fisher, *The Caucasian Storms Harlem*, in *The Norton Anthology of African American Literature,* ed. Henry Louis Gates Jr. and Nellie McKay (New York: Norton, 1997), p. 1194. Published online at <www.fishernews.org/fishworks/caucasian.htm>.

Page 46   Los Angeles, Mexico City and Prague: Mark Kurlansky, *1968: The Year That Rocked the World* (New York, Ballantine, 2004), p. 236.

Page 47   *Time* magazine's: James Graaf, "Streets of Fire," *Time*, November 5, 2005.

Page 47   Looking at the Asian scene: Boyd, *New H.N.I.C.*, p. 15.

Page 47   Meanwhile back in the old continent: Daara J, in an interview on NPR, May 20, 2005: "The first time we heard Grandmaster Flash rapping on a hip hop track, everybody was like, 'OK, we know this because this is tasso [the rhythmic oral history in Senegal]." <www.npr.org/templates/story/story.php?storyId=466>, accessed March 7, 2006.

Chapter Four: Faith-Based Cool

Page 49   "Jesus is just the best trip": Quoted in Charles Marsh, *Beloved Community: How Faith Shapes Social Justice, from the Civil Rights Movement to Today* (New York: Basic Books, 2005), p. 141; "Jesus is a Rebel": see REBEL brand Clothiers, <www.jesusisarebel.com/home.html>; Erwin McManus, quoted in <www.christianexaminer.com/Articles/Articles%20Mar05/Art_Mar05_09.html>.

Page 49   In the first century: Alan Johnson, *1 Corinthians*, IVP New Testament Commentaries (Downers Grove, Ill.: InterVarsity Press, 2004), p. 100.

Page 50   "It becomes impossible": Douglas Rushkoff, online content for *The Merchants of Cool*, Frontline/PBS, 2001, <www.pbs.org/wgbh/pages/frontline/shows/cool/etc/synopsis.html>, accessed November 30, 2005.

Page 53   When Roger Williams: Catherine Albanese, *America: Religion and Religions* (Belmont, Calif.: Wadsworth, 1992), p. 115.

Page 53   When a church in Georgia: John Leland, "The Punk-Christian Son of a Preacher Man," *The New York Times Magazine*, January 23, 2005.

Page 55   "Statistically speaking": John Jeremiah Sullivan, "Upon This Rock," *Gentlemen's Quarterly*, January 18, 2005; also published online, accessed November 30, 2005 at <http://men.style.com/gq/features/full?id=content_301>.

Page 56   "The deity-free": John Leland in *The New York Times*, May 18, 2004.

Page 57   The cause of justice: David Masson, "A Brief Life of Milton," in *Paradise Lost: Norton Critical Edition, Second Edition,* ed. Scott Elledge (New York: W. W. Norton, 1993), p. 334.

Page 57   The 1650s: Lacey Baldwin Smith, *This Realm of England: 1399 to 1688 (Sixth Ed.)* (Lexington, Mass.: D.C. Heath, 1992), p. 293.

Page 58   The new king: Masson, "Brief Life," p. 343.

Page 60   "reexamine Scripture": "Purpose Driven in Rwanda" in *Christianity Today*, October 2005, vol. 49, no. 10, p. 34.

Chapter Five: The Tao of Jesus

Page 67   Platzspitz Park: Platzspitz Park has since been closed; the experiment deemed a mixed result. The city's free sterile needle program did reduce HIV infection rates, and there was indeed little increase in rates of new addiction, but tens of thousands of addicts flooded the city from around the continent. Ultimately, Zurich's growing reputation as Europe's drugs capital, along with an increase in violence among drug dealers, was too much for the city. Platzspitz is not necessarily a good example against legalization, but those of us who lived in Zurich in the late 1980s and early 1990s gained a lot of insight into the daily realities of heroin addiction. Platzspitz is today once again a gem of a park in the heart of a beautiful city.

Page 68   male eating disorders: Bret E. Carroll, *American Masculinities: A Historical Encyclopedia* (Thousand Oaks, Calif.: Sage Publications, 2003), p. 58.

Page 68   female pornography consumption: Pamela Paul, *Pornified: How Pornography Is Transforming Our Lives, Our Relationships, and Our Families* (New York: Times Books, 2005), p. 111.

Page 69   "Transgression simply means": Lars Svendsen, *A Philosophy of Boredom* (London: Reaktion Books, 2005), p. 72.

Page 71   "God's reign descends": Allen Mitsuo Wakabayashi, *Kingdom Come: How Jesus Wants to Change the World* (Downers Grove, Ill.: InterVarsity Press, 2003), pp. 30-31.

Page 76   William Seymour: D. Jeffrey Bingham, *Pocket History of the Church* (Downers Grove, Ill.: InterVarsity Press, 2002), p. 147.

Page 77   "grounded in the groundless mystery": Cornel West, *The Courage to Hope* (Boston: Beacon Press, 1999), p. 228.

Page 77   "The idea of heaven": James Cone, "Calling the Oppressors to Account," in *The Courage to Hope*, ed. Quinton Dixie and Cornel West (Boston: Beacon Press, 1999), p. 76.

Chapter Six: Reenchantment

Page 81   It depicted: Table 4, Population of the United States, As Native and Foreign-Born, 1870 *US Census Bureau*, accessed on November 30, 2005 at <www2.census.gov/prod2/decennial/documents/1870a-10.pdf>.

Page 83   "mechanized petrification": Max Weber, *The Protestant Ethic and the Spirit of Capitalism*, (New York: Routledge, 1992), p. 182.

Page 84   Practitioners can play: Philip Jenkins, *Dream Catchers: How Mainstream America Discovered Native Spirituality* (London: Oxford, 2004).

Page 86   "One should live well": John Patrick Donelly, S.J., and Roland Teske, S.J., *Robert Bellarmine: Spiritual Writings* (Mahwah, N.J.: Paulist, 1989), p. 235.

Page 88   "the contracting parties": Walter Roehrs and Martin Franzmann, *Concordia Self-Study Commentary* (St. Louis: Concordia, 1979).

Chapter Seven: Compassion

Page 100   "On the contrary": Henri Nouwen, Donald McNeill and Douglas Morrison, *Compassion: A Reflection on the Christian Life* (New York: Image Books/Doubleday, 1982), p. 27.

Page 102   Equality of sin: Miroslav Volf, *Exclusion and Embrace: A Theological Explora-*

tion of Identity, Otherness, and Reconciliation (Nashville: Abingdon, 1996), p. 82.

Page 104   Pornography, according to: Pamela Paul, *Pornified: How Pornography Is Transforming Our Lives, Our Relationships, and Our Families* (New York: Times Books, 2005), p. 89.

Page 105   "It's not easy being a soldier": Corner Pocket, "Stay in Step," distributed through *Download.com*, accessed November 30, 2005 at <music .download.com/cornerpocket/3600-8538_32-100631749.html>.

Page 106   "The blues present": Craig Werner, *A Change Is Gonna Come: Music, Race, and the Soul of America* (New York: Penguin, 1999), pp. 69-70.

Page 106   "It's too much for you": 4th25, "Reality Check," distributed through Apple iTunes, accessed November 30, 2005 at <http://phobos.apple.com/ WebObjects/MZStore.woa/wa/viewAlbum?id=65443499&s=143441>.

Page 107   "Many of the returning soldiers": Ridley Usherwood, interviewed by Paul Grant, "Veterans at Your Doorstep," *Urbana.org*, November 2, 2005 <www.urbana.org/_articles.cfm?RecordId=928>.

Chapter Eight: Deep Uncool

Page 113   We are not liberated: When we listen to others' stories, we are inevitably surprised by the events they feel most passionately about. In 2006, Americans were vaguely aware of European anger toward America, and most journalists assumed the anger came from the Iraq war. But top on the new German foreign minister's agenda in his first visit to Washington was the CIA's alleged transportation of terrorist suspects across European airspace. Europeans were ready to kick countries out of the European Union, they were so angry, but in the United States the events went largely unremarked.

Chapter Nine: Beyond Cool

Page 121   "Children of the Kingdom": Bob Morris, "At Work in Us," Urbana.org, December 5, 2005 <www.urbana.org/wtoday.ephesians.cfm?article#37>.

Page 122   Christian hope is thus "hipi": See chapter two, page 31: the word *hip* derives from the West African Wolof word *hipi*, meaning "to see beyond; to see farther." *Hipi* was a cultural import to the new world during slavery.

Page 123   "'Hope' in common English usage": Morris, "At Work in Us."

Page 123   "[Today's humans]": Norman Mailer, "The White Negro," *IV Dissent*, Spring 1957 <http://xroads.virginia.edu/~DRBR2/whitenegro.html>.

Page 125   "America was the land": Garrison Keillor, *Lake Wobegon Days* (New York: Viking Penguin, 1985), p. 65.

Page 126   When white people: For more on ethnic choices faced by immigrants, see Noel Ignatiev, *How the Irish Became White* (New York: Routledge, 1995).

Page 129   "A strip of land": Craig Van Gelder, *The Essence of the Church: A Community Created by the Spirit* (Grand Rapids: Baker, 2000), pp. 99-100.

Page 133   Over the decades: In a recent *Dallas Morning News* article, for instance, the pastor of a middle-class African American church proudly announces, "The time for the whooping, the jumping-up-and-down pastor is over." (Linda Stewart Ball, "Counting Their Blessings in the Suburbs," June 29, 2005).

Page 133   "Messiness in worship": Alex Gee, in interview with author.

Uncool 2.0

There are as many conclusions to be drawn from these pages as there are readers. Join in; let's have a wide-ranging conversation about moving forward together as a healthy church.

Chapter One   How have you tried, succeeded or failed at being cool? Share your story. http://uncoolbook.blogspot.com/2006/01/discovering-cool.html

Chapter Two   What's the difference between rejecting cool and living beyond it? http://uncoolbook.blogspot.com/2006/02/performing-our-rebellion.html

Chapter Three   Cool is about broken relationships, from race to gender to generation gaps. Christianity is about reconciliation. Share your story. http://uncool book.blogspot.com/2006/03/reconciliation-hurts.html

Chapter Four   Was Jesus really a rebel? http://uncoolbook.blogspot.com/2006/04/rebel-jesus.html

Chapter Five   In this chapter I tell a story of leaving a party as someone was getting manhandled. What should I have done? What should anyone have done? http://uncoolbook.blogspot.com/2006/05/orchard street.html

Chapter Six   Belonging to the church is harder in practice than in theory. Share your story. http://uncoolbook.blogspot.com/2006/06/belonging.html

Chapter Seven   Is compassion really the opposite of cool? Discuss. http://uncool book.blogspot.com/2006/07/compassion.html

Chapter Eight   I argue that cool belongs nowhere near Jesus' witnesses in a hurting world. Discuss. http://uncoolbook.blogspot.com/2006/08/missionary-cool.html

Chapter Nine   Stir your memory pot: What family experiences do you want to reclaim for the church? http://uncoolbook.blogspot.com/2006/09/stir-memory-pot.html

Beyond   Show and Tell! Links from the Uncool blog will help you continue the conversation. Join Uncoolbook groups at Flickr and Youtube. Tag the uncool world at del.ício.us. Take the discussion further at the Myspace Uncool group and the Xanga Uncool blogring. http://uncool-book.blogspot.com/2006/09/uncool-20.html.